# GRAPHIC MASTERS

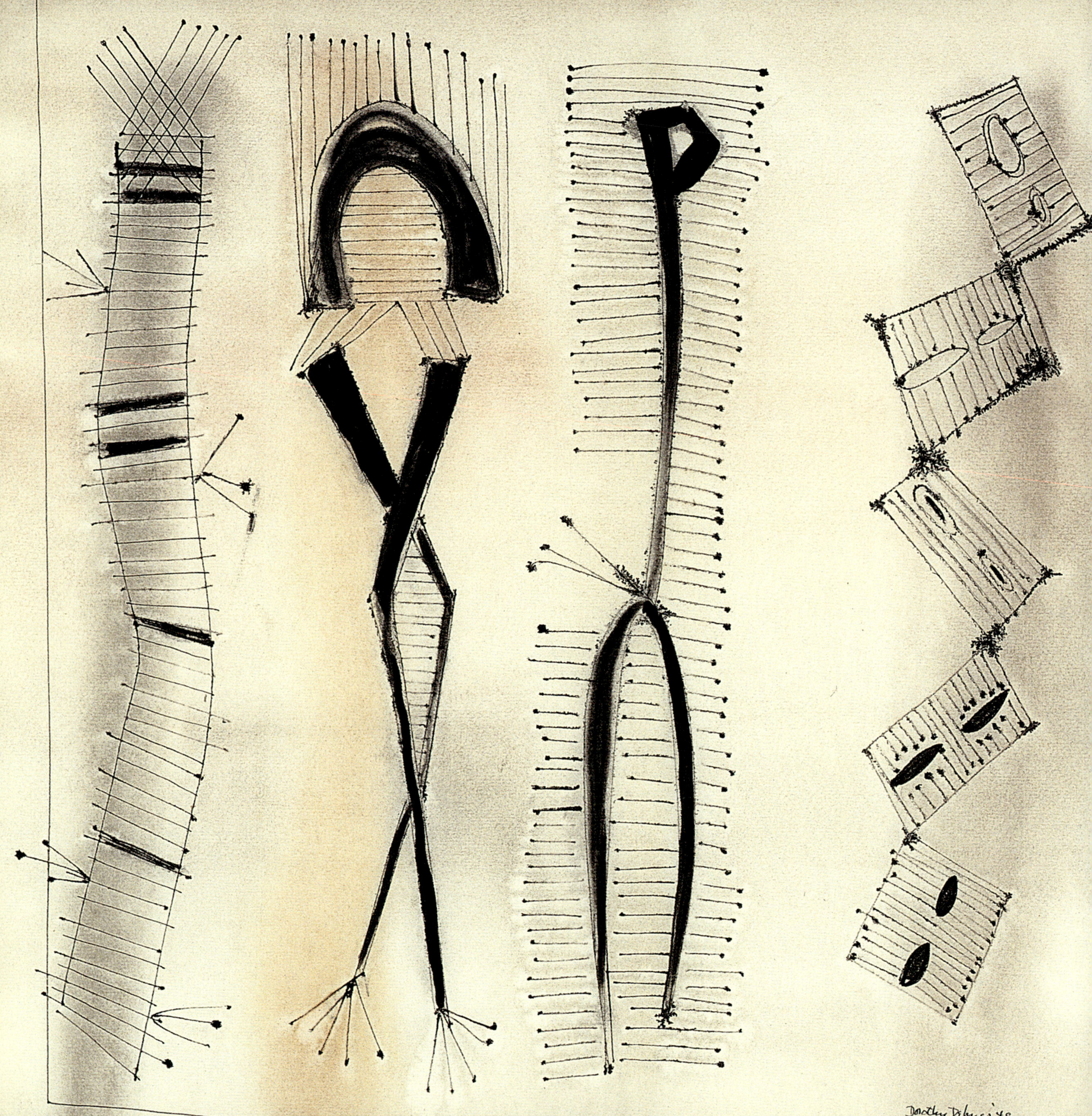
Dorothy Dehner '49

# GRAPHIC MASTERS

*Highlights from the Smithsonian American Art Museum*

*Joann Moser*

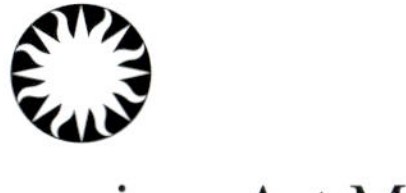

Smithsonian American Art Museum

Graphic Masters: Highlights from the Smithsonian American Art Museum

By Joann Moser

Chief, Publications: Theresa J. Slowik
Designers: Karen Siatras, Steve Bell
Editor: Timothy D. Wardell

Library of Congress Cataloging-in-Publication Data

Moser, Joann.
Graphic masters : highlights from the Smithsonian American Art Museum / Joann Moser.
p. cm. — (Highlights from the Smithsonian American Art Museum)
Includes index.
ISBN 0-937311-56-1 (pbk.)
1. Drawing, American—20th century—Catalogs.
2. Drawing—Washington, D.C.—Catalogs.
3. Smithsonian American Art Museum—Catalogs.
I. Title: Highlights from the Smithsonian American Art Museum. II. Smithsonian American Art Museum. III. Title. IV. Series.
NC108 .M59 2003
741.973'074'753—dc21

2002154513

Printed and bound in Spain

First printing, 2003
1 2 3 4 5 6 7 8 9 / 08 07 06 05 04 03 02 01


First published in 2003



Cover: Wayne Thiebaud, *Neapolitan Meringue,* 1986–99, pastel over lithograph. Smithsonian American Art Museum, Gift of Warren Unna, Terry and Margaret Stent, and the Thiebaud Family, and museum purchase in honor of Nan Tucker McEvoy (see page 94)

Frontispiece: Dorothy Dehner, *The People in the Story; Bolton Landing* (detail), 1949, pen and ink and watercolor wash. Smithsonian American Art Museum, Museum purchase (see page 36)

*Graphic Masters* is one of five exhibitions presented as *Highlights from the Smithsonian American Art Museum,* touring the nation through 2005.

Generous support from the Sara Roby Foundation has made possible this publication.

# Foreword

Working in a museum, I have come to appreciate the joys of repeated encounters and easy intimacy with works of surpassing tranquility or great power. I also love the surprise of the unexpected when I see something new or challenging in another museum. Visitors here and abroad share these same experiences, encountering artworks as familiar friends in settings close to home or unanticipated discoveries in different places.

The Smithsonian American Art Museum is the nation's museum dedicated exclusively to the art and artists of the United States. The collections trace the country's story in art spanning three centuries, and its in-depth resources offer opportunities to understand that story better. While our main building undergoes extensive refurbishment, we have a great opportunity to share our finest artworks with everyone across the nation.

From 2003 through 2005, five traveling shows will feature four hundred works, including modern African American art, landscape photography, master drawings, contemporary crafts, and pre-1850 quilts. Readying this wave of ambassadors has called upon the talents and enterprising spirit of the entire staff, especially the curators, conservators, registrars, and editors. I would like to thank all who have worked so hard to make possible this ongoing initiative to share our collections during the renovation period. We are also grateful for the support of the Smithsonian Special Exhibitions Fund and numerous supporters as well as to the several dozen American museums who will graciously host these traveling exhibitions.

*Graphic Masters* celebrates the extraordinary variety and accomplishment of American artists' works on paper. Exceptional watercolors, pastels, and drawings from the 1860s through the 1990s reveal the central importance of works on paper for American artists, both as studies for creations in other media and as finished works of art. Even as works on paper became larger and more finished, competing in scale with easel paintings, they retain a sense of the artist's hand, the immediacy of a thought made visible.

We invite you to revisit our collections as familiar friends when they are installed in the museum's beautifully restored building in Washington, a historic artwork in its own right. There you will encounter expanded spaces for exciting special exhibitions and for the permanent collection's showcasing, including the Luce Foundation Center for American Art. This open-storage facility will house five thousand paintings, sculptures, and craft and folk objects previously inaccessible to the public. A new publicly visible conservation lab will reveal the complex processes of restoring artworks, while an array of public programming and educational resources, onsite and online, will also enhance the experiences of visitors and researchers alike. We look forward to welcoming you to the new Smithsonian American Art Museum.

Elizabeth Broun
*The Margaret and Terry Stent Director*
*Smithsonian American Art Museum*

**ROBERT ARNESON**

1930–1992

## *Feeling Pushed*

1977
chalk, pencil, and crayon
41 ½ x 29 ⅞ in.
Smithsonian American Art Museum, Gift of Mr. and Mrs. Kurt Olden

*Feeling Pushed* captures Robert Arneson at an especially stressful moment in his life. Two years earlier, he had been diagnosed with cancer, possibly caused by the chemicals contained in his art materials. He underwent surgery and was required to return to the hospital numerous times. Despite this serious threat to his health, Arneson injects humor into his self-portrait, even vulgarity. His face seems to be pushed up against a piece of transparent glass that flattens his nose into a piggish snout, while his wild hair and wrinkled features express the tension and anxiety that characterize his state of mind. The artist appears like a specimen prepared for a microscopic examination. Arneson frequently turned to self-portraiture as a means to examine his relationship with the world, expressing serious thought and difficult emotional content through the filter of a humorous mask.

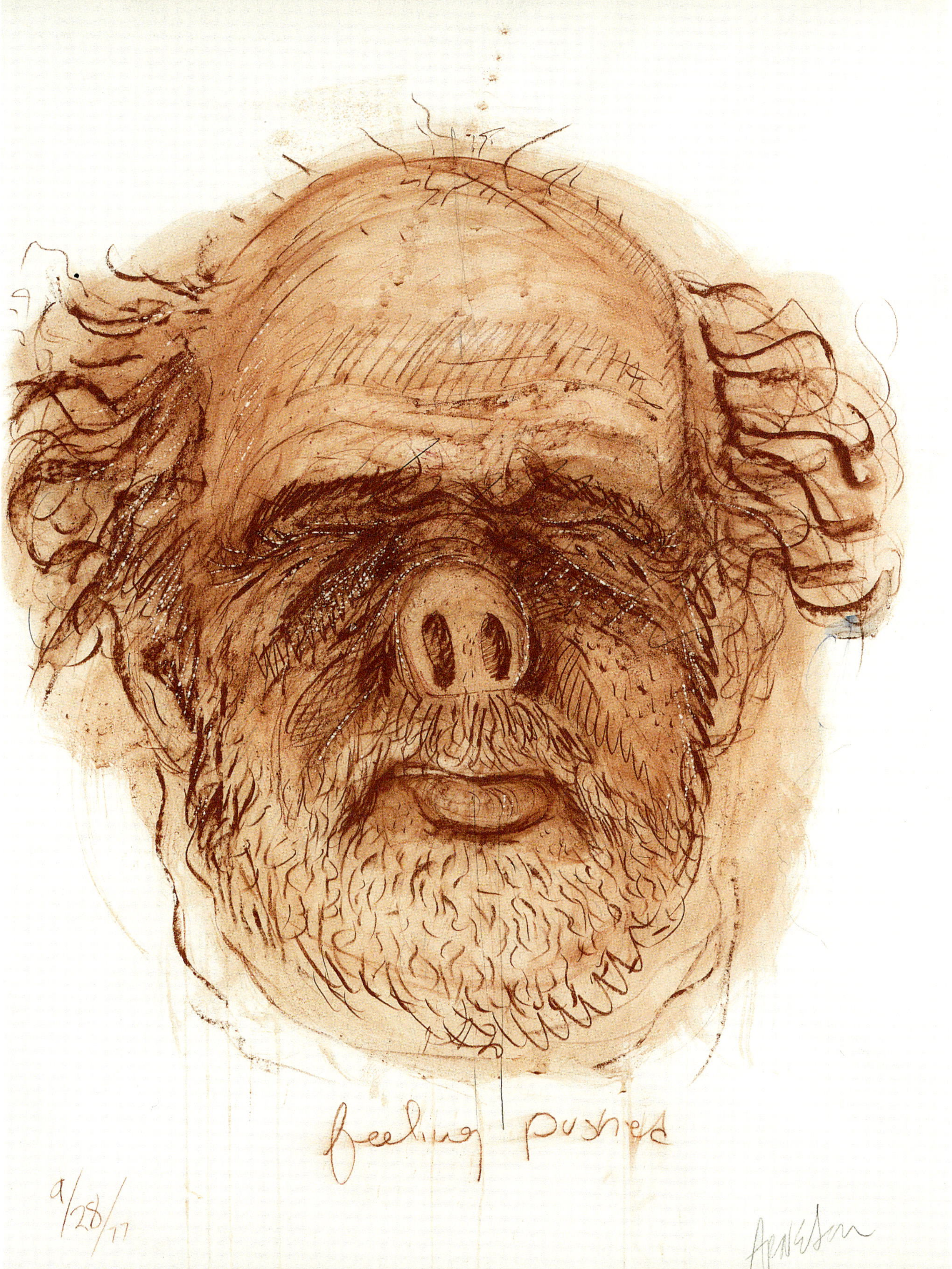
feeling pushed
9/28/77
Arneson

**EDWARD MITCHELL BANNISTER**

1828 Canada–1901 USA

## *Landscape with Path through Forest*

after 1870
chalk and charcoal
17 1/4 x 11 3/8 in.
Smithsonian American Art Museum,
Gift of Abraham and Faye Adler

Edward Mitchell Bannister's *Landscape with Path through Forest* gives little clue to the artist's African American background. The serene, intimate view of a forest path, with light filtering gently through the trees, suggests a cathedral-like space, a hushed setting for the contemplation of nature. The fallen tree trunk in the foreground, however, acts as a barrier—suggesting that the artist's entry into this privileged space is blocked.

Bannister settled in Boston as a young man and later moved to Providence, Rhode Island, where he spent the better part of his career. He had access to art in museums and private homes in these two cities, but equally sought inspiration in nature. This scene indicates the artist's reverence for the solace it offered. Early in his career, he received acclaim as a portrait painter but is now better remembered for his landscape paintings and drawings.

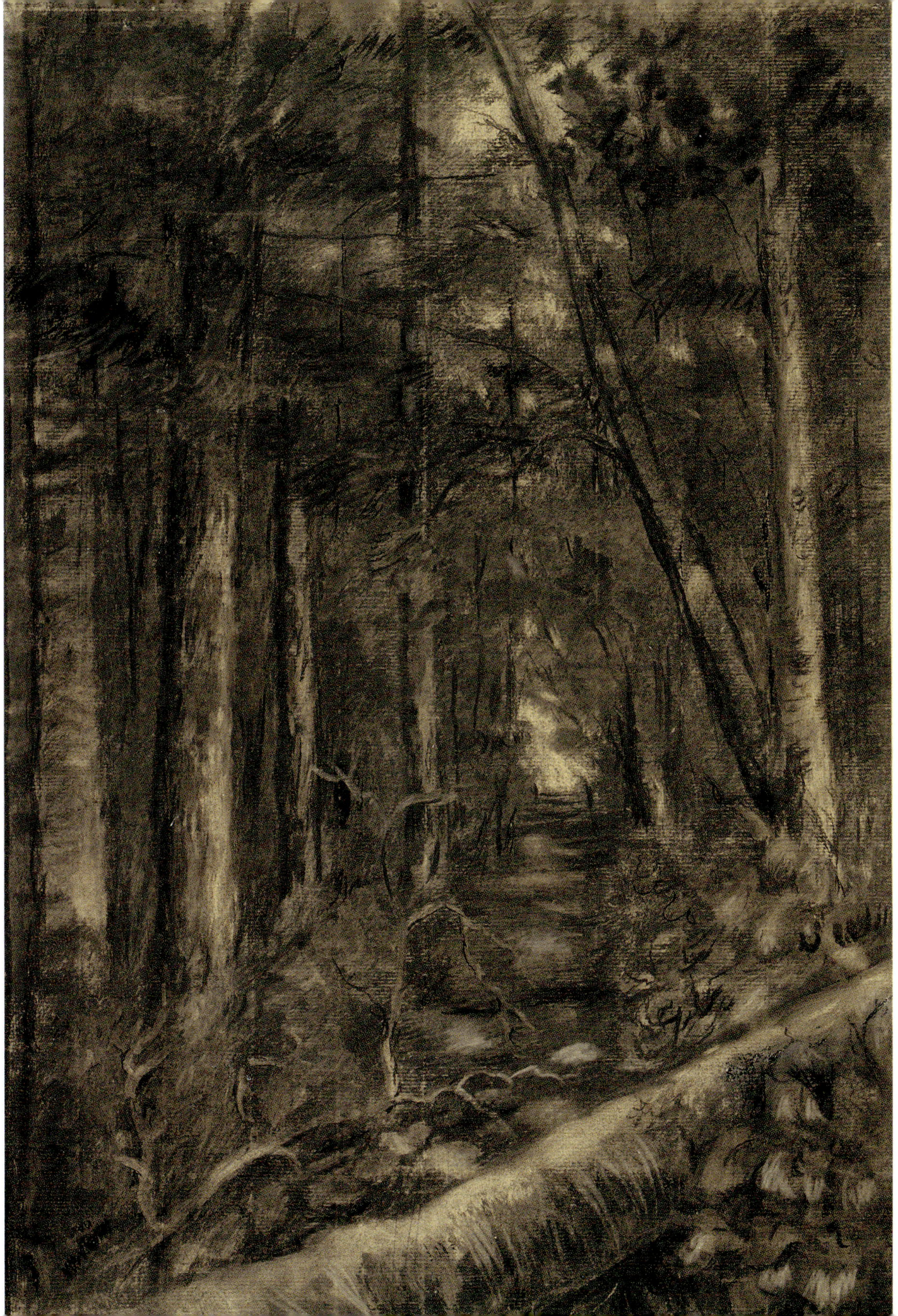

**WILL BARNET**
born 1911

# *Study for Self-Portrait*

1982–83
charcoal on vellum
with traces of
colored pencil
47 ½ x 38 in.
Smithsonian
American Art
Museum,
Gift of the artist

Will Barnet has relied heavily on his own family as models. In *Study for Self-Portrait,* the painting on the easel behind the artist shows his wife, Elena, and their cat, cradled on her shoulder as if it were a child. Relationships—between people, between man and animal, between man's interior and exterior selves, between art and nature—have been the pivotal concern in his art. Here, in addition to his relationship with his wife and cat, he investigates his own identity as an artist.

Through seven decades, Barnet has created a distinguished body of paintings, prints, and drawings founded on the same humanistic values that have characterized memorable art of the past. He combines realism and abstraction in a distinctive expression, deriving inspiration from everyday life, mythology, literature, ancient and contemporary art. Barnet's subjects convey universal values in a language founded on monumental form and classical order.

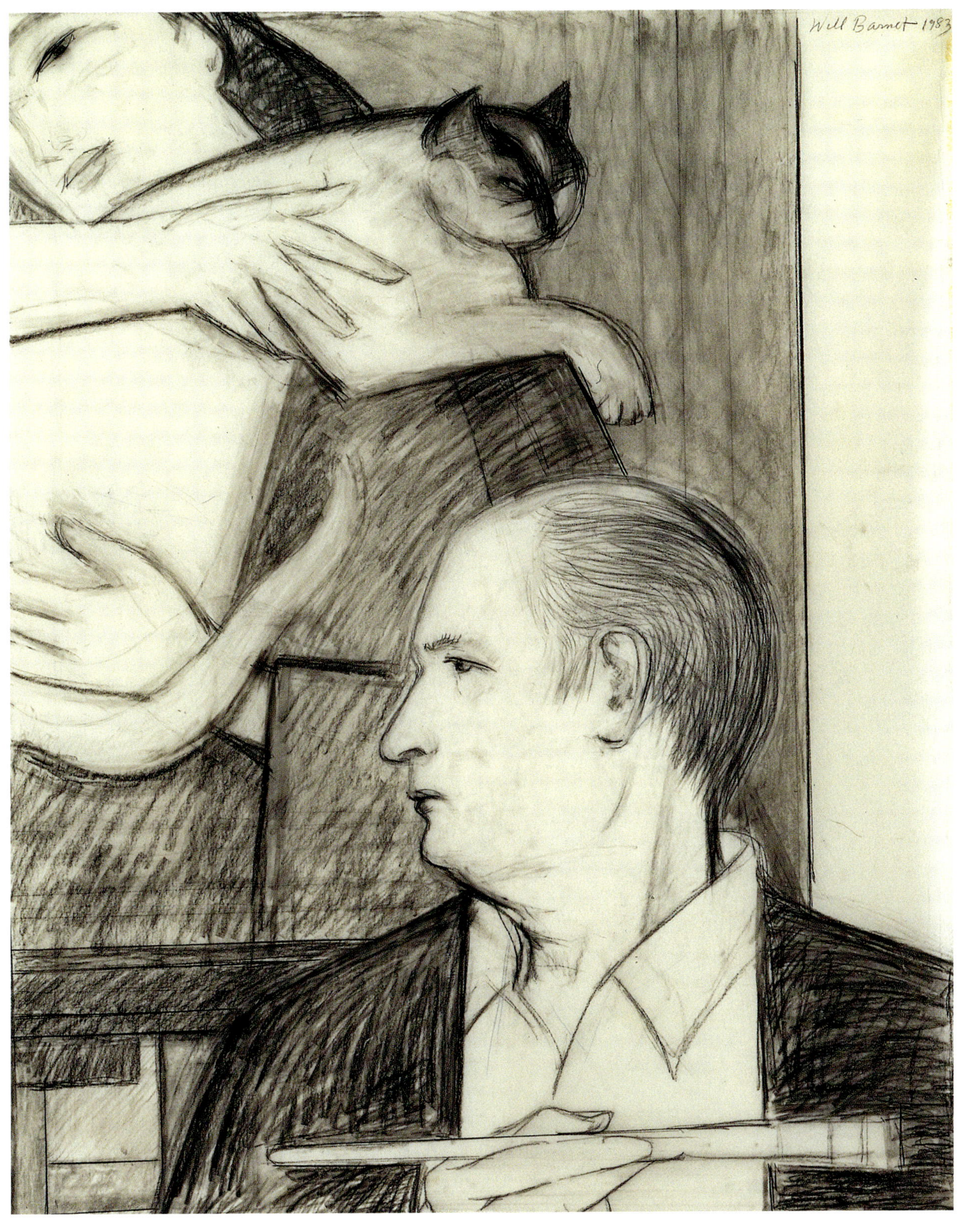
Will Barnet 1983

**JENNIFER BARTLETT**

born 1941

# *Study for Swimmers Atlanta: Seaweed*

1979
watercolor, enamel, pen and ink, and pencil
20 x 20 in.
Smithsonian American Art Museum, Transfer from the General Services Administration, Art-in-Architecture Program

*Swimmers Atlanta* is a nine-painting mural commissioned for a federal court lobby in Atlanta, Georgia. To prepare for this ambitious commission, Jennifer Bartlett made watercolor studies, such as *Seaweed,* for each painting. She then transferred these drawings freehand to much larger surfaces to complete the final mural.

Bartlett evokes different phenomena an ocean swimmer might encounter: icebergs, eels, whirlpools, buoys, flares, rocks, boats, bottles, and seaweed. Swimmers and ocean waters are recurring themes for Bartlett, who grew up near the ocean's edge on a peninsula in Long Beach, California. Her symbol of the human presence is a simple, featureless ellipse. Each composition has two parts, often in direct opposition to each other, such as day/night, rain/sun, or choppy/smooth. In *Seaweed* the left half shows lozenge-shaped forms floating horizontally on a calm sea, while the right half suggests choppy water tossing the forms in all directions. In contrast to the cool blues of the water, the reddish threads of seaweed drift alongside the swimmers or entangle them in the more active waters.

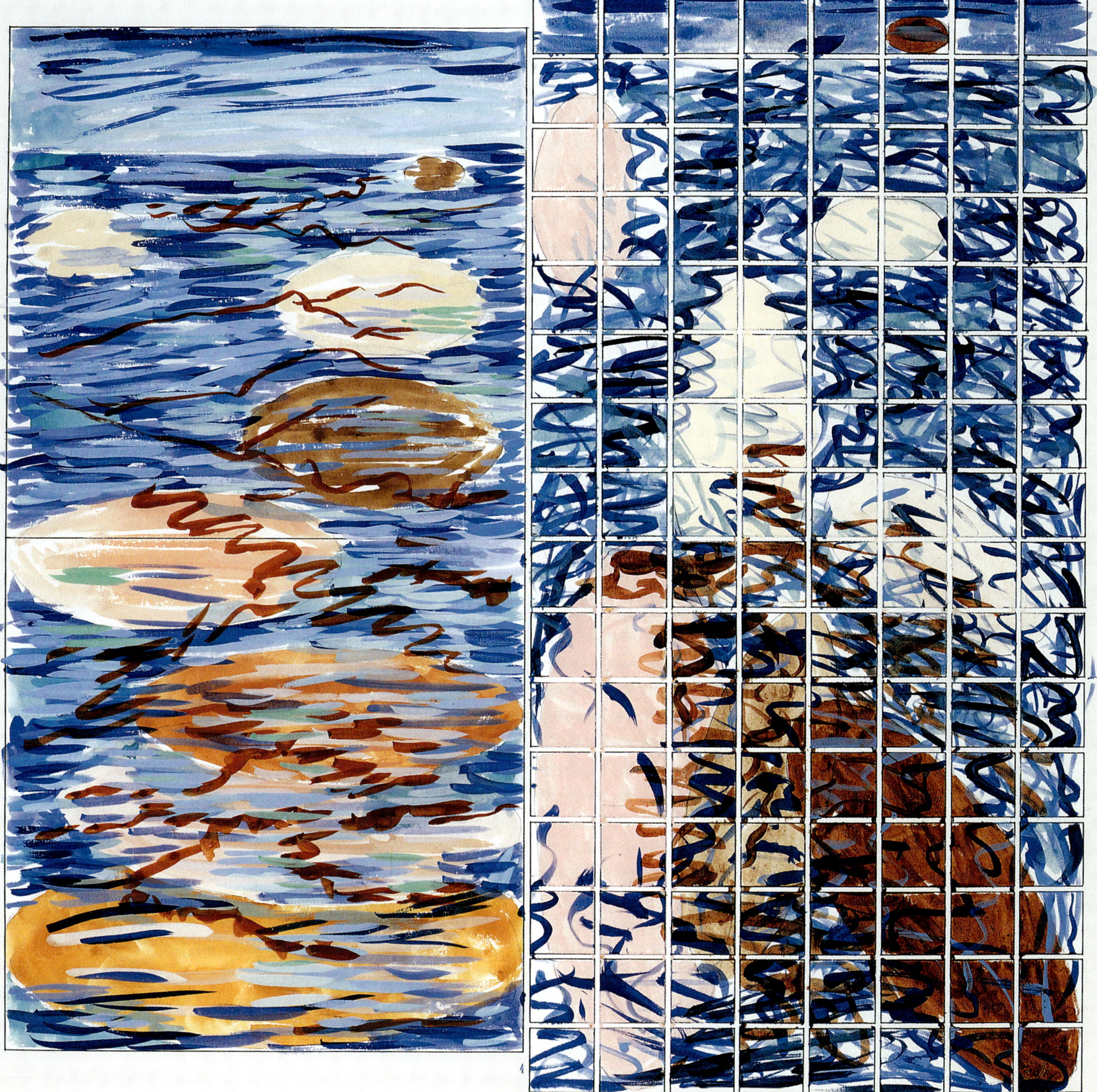

**MEL BOCHNER**

born 1940

# *Skeleton (Skew)*

1979–81
charcoal
30 x 50 in.
Smithsonian
American Art
Museum

In 1978 Mel Bochner began a series of "skeleton" drawings in which the outlines of primary shapes were interconnected to create composite, indeterminate forms that seem to expand over a large, horizontal space. *Skeleton (Skew)* is one of the most highly developed drawings of this series, in which Bochner worked out the major elements of the abstract vocabulary he has continued to use. He explores how simple forms may be used to disclose complexity. As in his earlier drawings, Bochner exploits the tension between the two major shapes to create an explosive visual energy. The triangular and trapezoidal forms suggest an orderly and rational structure, at the same time Bochner celebrates expressiveness and spontaneity. The shifting and lightly erased lines create intricate webs that animate the forms with a sense of time and organic locomotion.

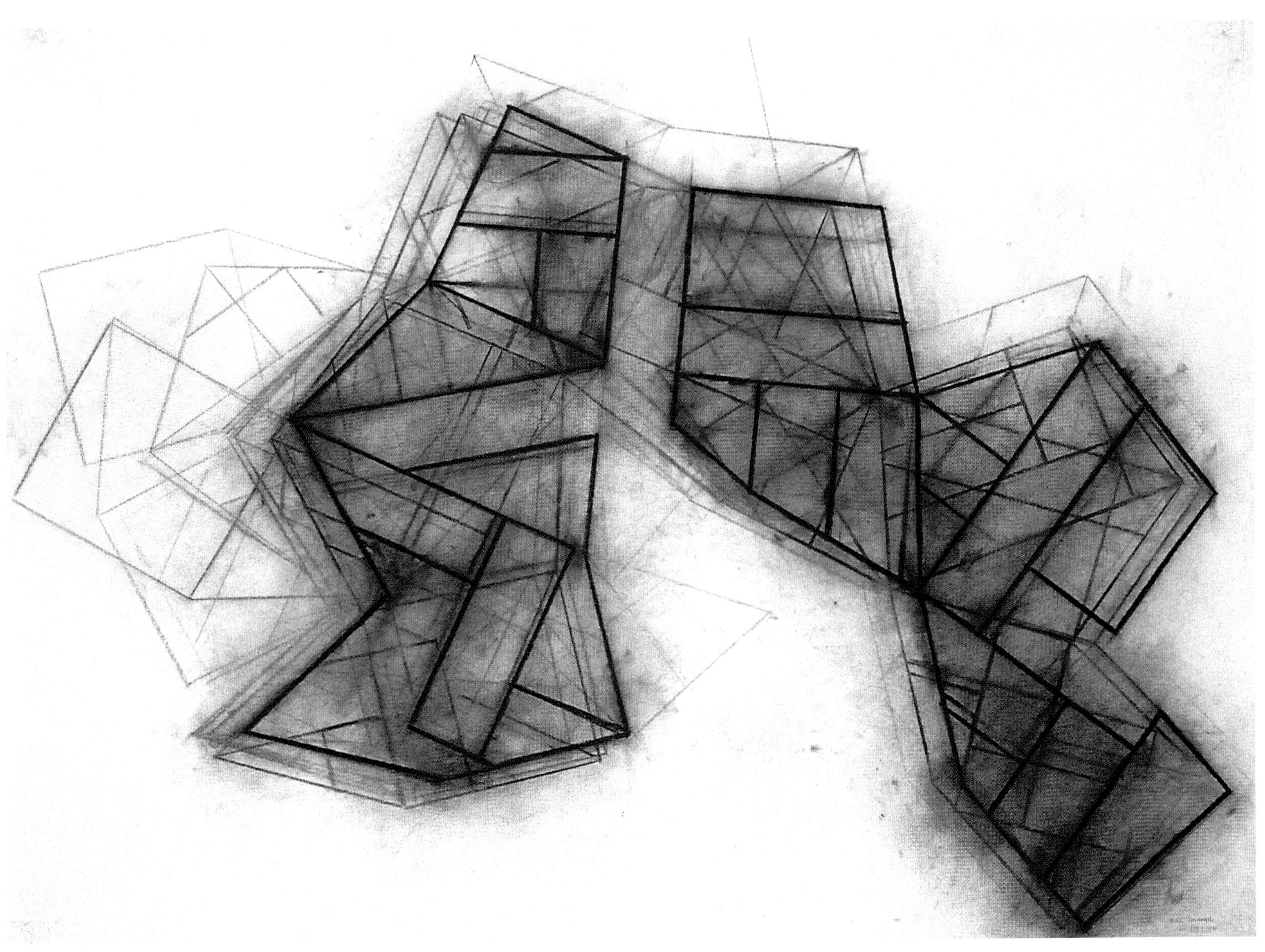

**CAROLYN BRADY**

born 1937

## *August Breakfast/Maine*

1997
watercolor
28 x 37 in.
Smithsonian American Art Museum, Gift of Nancy Hoffman, Rebecca Hoffman-Greenwald and Peter Greenwald

Carolyn Brady arranged this still life composition in her studio on Vinalhaven Island, Maine. She photographed the arrangement, projected the image onto a large sheet of paper, and made a faint, quick pencil sketch of it. As she painted the forms with transparent watercolors, she continually referred to the large color photograph and, rather than "correct for the lens," she incorporated those distortions introduced by the camera lens into her final work. The clear focus of the foreground contrasts dramatically with the soft focus of the background, with relatively little transition in the middle ground. As a result, the composition seems mysteriously fragmented and inconsistent with our visual perception, introducing an element of tension. Brady refers to herself as an "abstract realist," acknowledging the important role contradiction plays in her presentation of scenes from daily life.

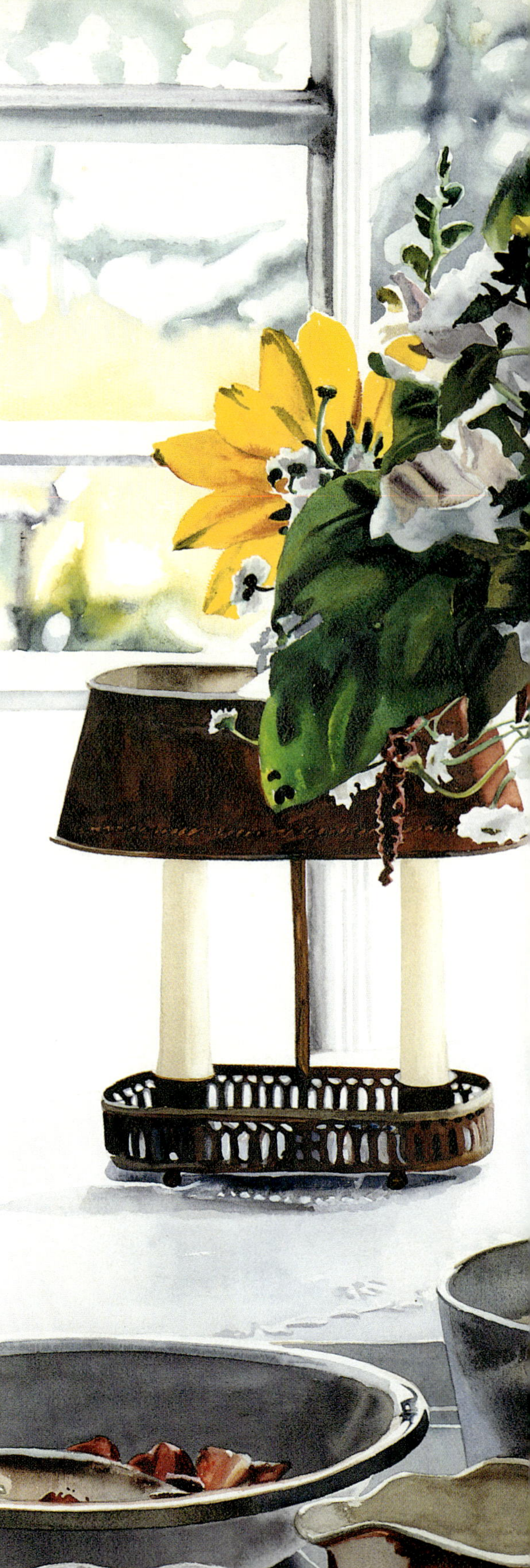

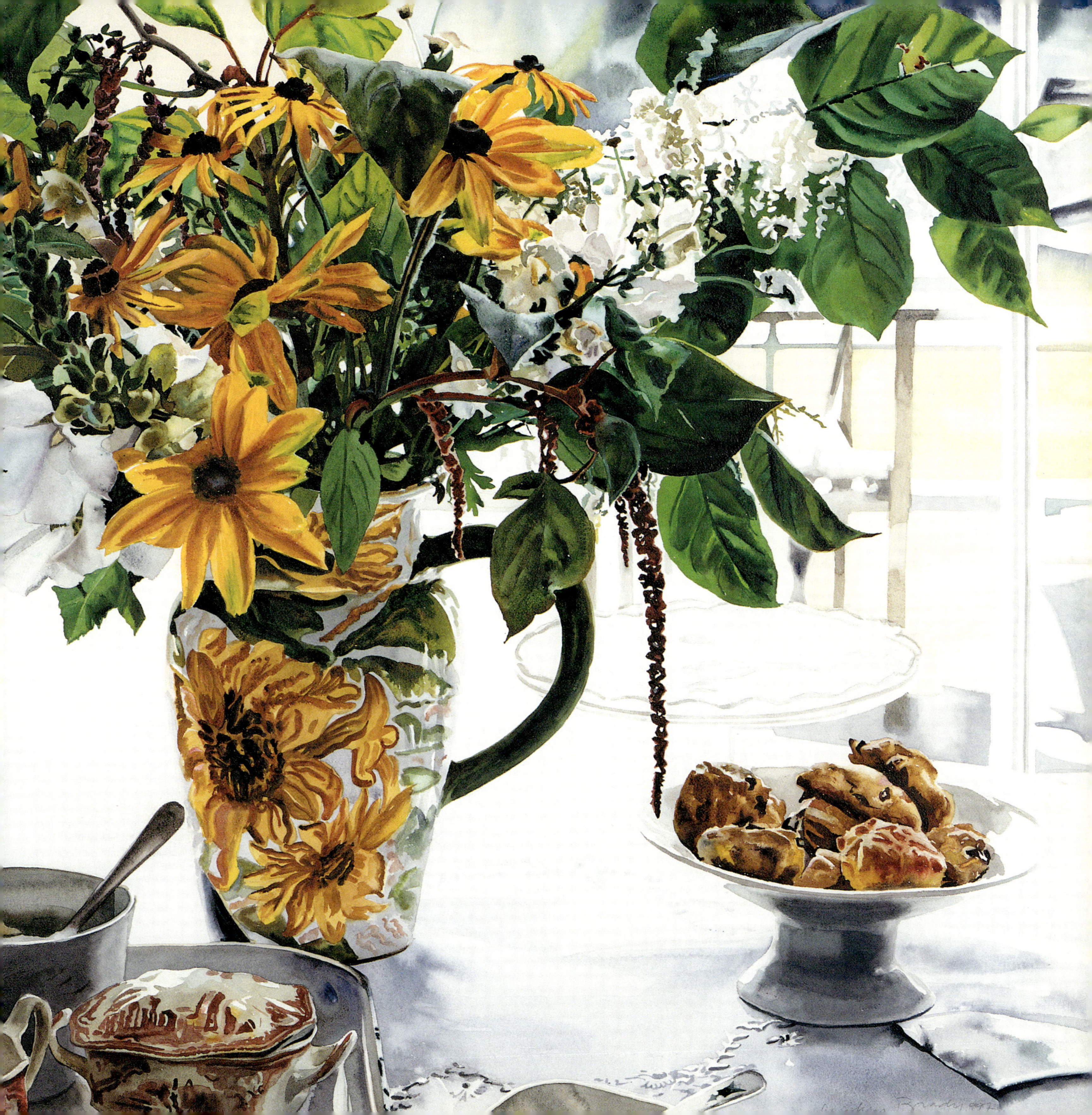

**ROMAINE BROOKS**

1874 Italy–1970 France

## *It Makes the Dead Sing*

about 1930
charcoal and pencil
18 ⅝ x 12 ¼ in.
Smithsonian American Art Museum,
Gift of the artist

After a short but successful career as a portrait painter to European high society, Romaine Brooks became obsessed with her privacy in the 1930s and withdrew from contact with most other people. She wrote a memoir of her life with a cruel, often-absent mother and demented brother, which she titled *No Pleasant Memories.* She planned to illustrate the book with evocative, linear fantasies that suggest more than they reveal. *It Makes the Dead Sing* is one of the most complex and accomplished of those images. A hooded, robed figure gathers tortured souls to its bosom, a lugubrious chorale of singing and wailing figures. More than a personal lamentation, it represents a universal, apocalyptic vision.

Brooks saw these drawings as expressions of her unconscious mind and said, "these drawings should be read." She asserted that she had no idea what would evolve as she poised her pencil over the sheet of paper. Charged with emotion, mystery, and poetry, her spare drawings recall the symbolic, literary visions of Edgar Allen Poe, Oscar Wilde, and Paul Valéry.

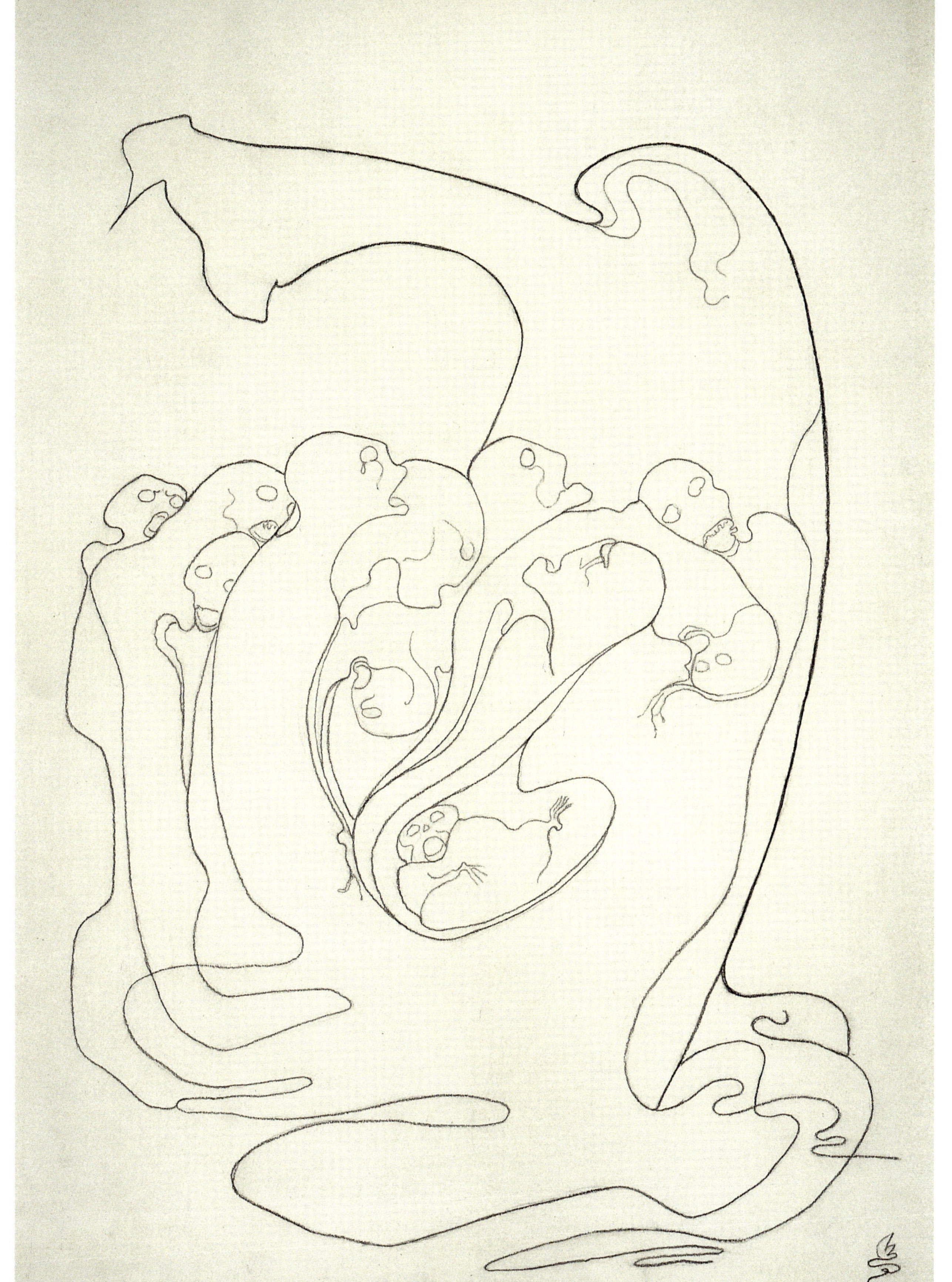

**CHARLES BURCHFIELD**

1893–1967

## *Lightning and Thunder at Night*

1920
watercolor and charcoal
19 x 26 in.
Smithsonian American Art Museum, Gift of Charles Rand Penney

Burchfield's creative process incorporated his dream life, with compositions such as this one recalling childhood fears and nightmares. His imagery remained strongly rooted in natural phenomena with references to sound as important as visual forms. He used landscape's symbolic associations to convey his moods. *Lightning and Thunder at Night* captures the dramatic effects of noise and light accompanying a violent storm. Shrill claps and intense flashes of lightning pierce the night sky with fearsome resonance. This storm seems to have a sinister spirit of its own.

Burchfield's early training emphasized watercolor painting, and he preferred working in this medium to painting in oil. After he began to show in New York in the 1920s, he enlarged the size of his watercolors so that they could compete on a more equal footing with oil paintings by other artists.

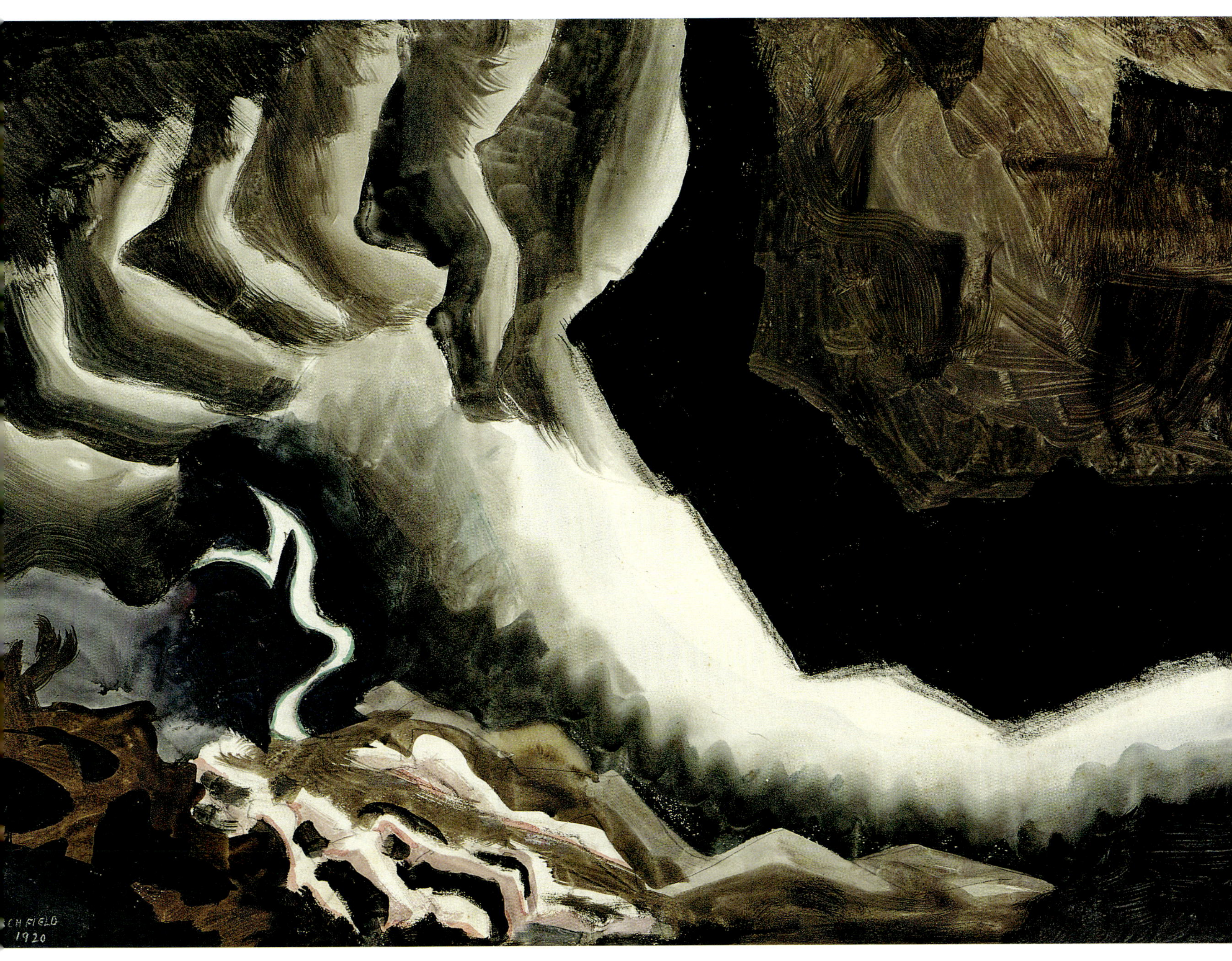
CHFIELD
1920

**PAUL CADMUS**

1904–1999

# *Preliminary sketch for Subway Symphony*

1973
pencil, casein, crayon, and chalk
21 5/8 x 40 in.
Smithsonian American Art Museum, Gift of the Sara Roby Foundation

A longtime subway rider himself, Cadmus transformed the everyday experience of commuting into a living Inferno, with figures of every shape, size, class, and ethnic group crammed together in their underground journey. For this microcosm of the larger New York melting pot, Cadmus explained how he chose his models: "Ugliness. Ugliness rules there. I will leave out the mediocre, the inbetweens. To distill an altar of essence I must select only the perfect petals, the most hellish." Yet this vision of social hideousness recalls the artistic tradition of finding redeeming value in ugliness. Cadmus exaggerated his subjects with wit and empathy, and captured the individuality of each figure.

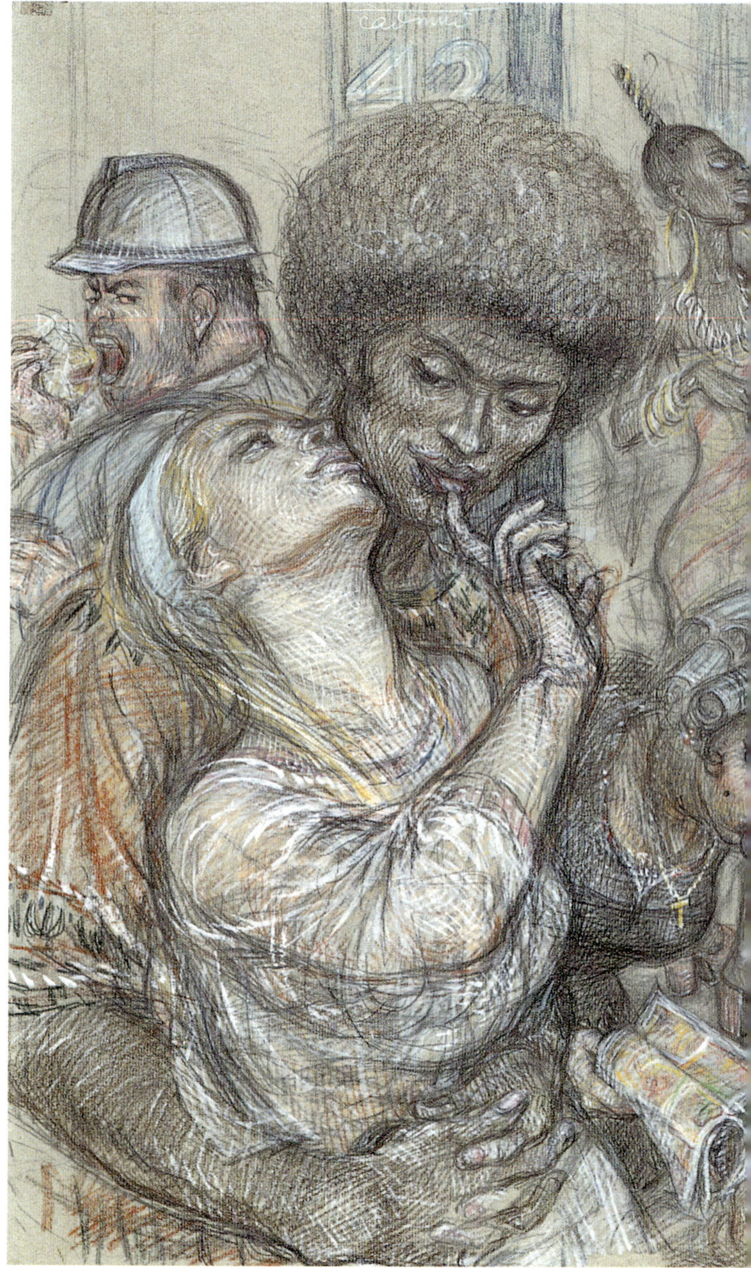

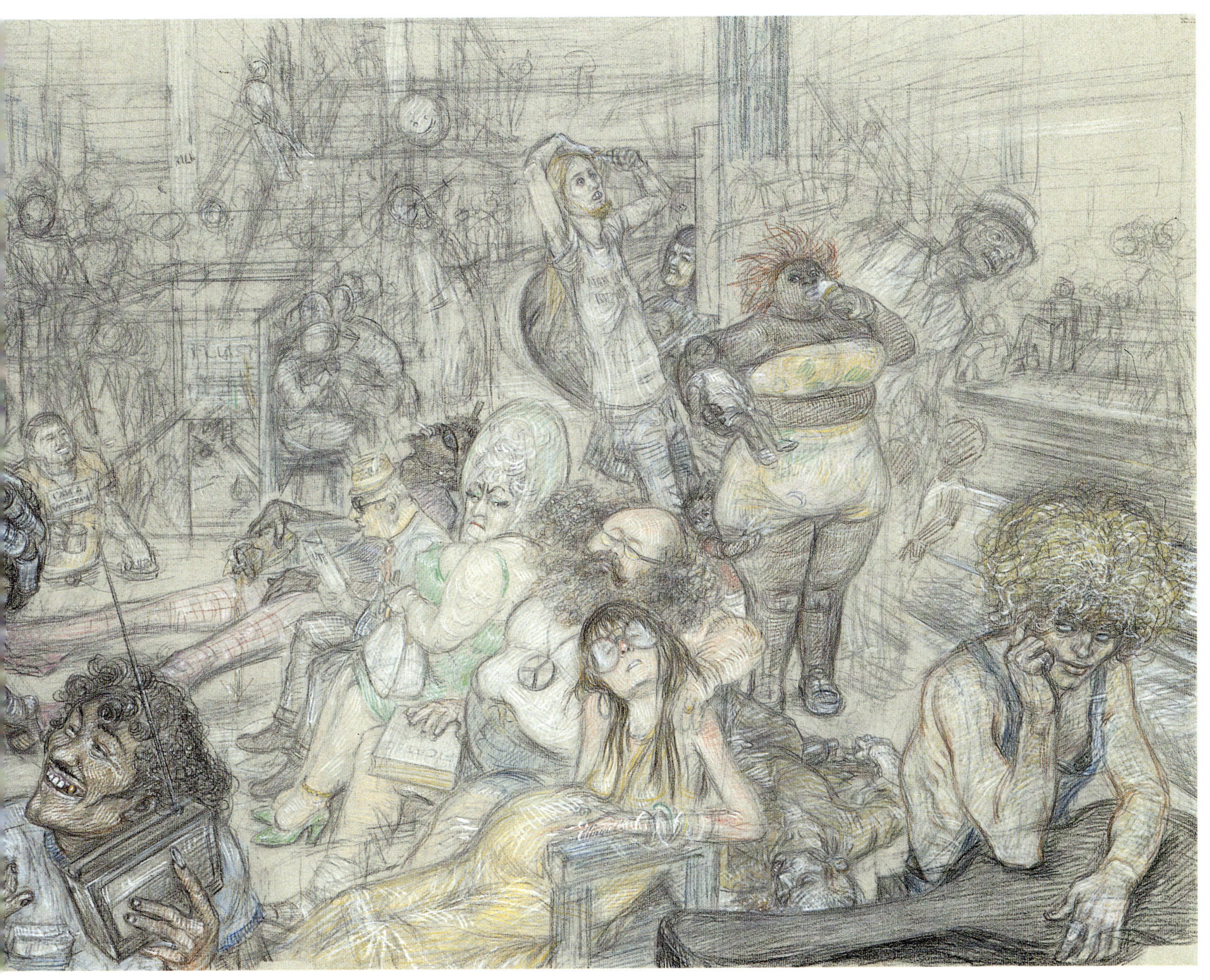

**WILLIAM MERRITT CHASE**

1849–1916

## *Terrace, Prospect Park*

about 1887
pastel
9 3/8 x 13 7/8 in.
Smithsonian American Art Museum, Gift of John Gellatly

William Merritt Chase drew *Terrace, Prospect Park* at an important moment in his career. After years of traveling back and forth to Europe and developing his skills as a portrait painter, in 1886 Chase married Alice Gerson and settled down in Brooklyn. He turned his attention to the natural world around him, especially Prospect Park in Brooklyn and Central Park in Manhattan.

This interest in his immediate surroundings coincided with an important exhibition of French impressionists in New York City, organized by the Parisian art dealer Paul Durand-Ruel. Under their influence, Chase brightened his palette, shortened his brushstrokes, and began to work out-of-doors.

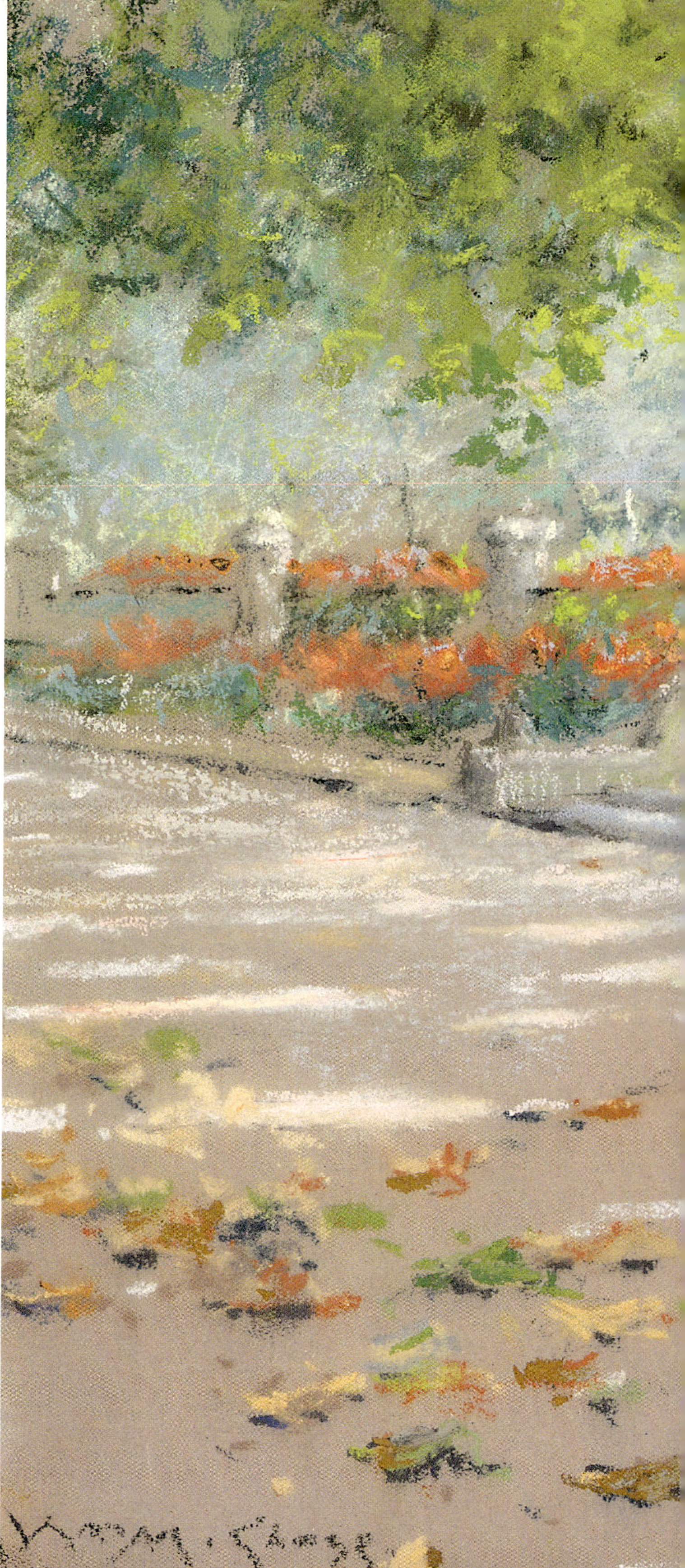

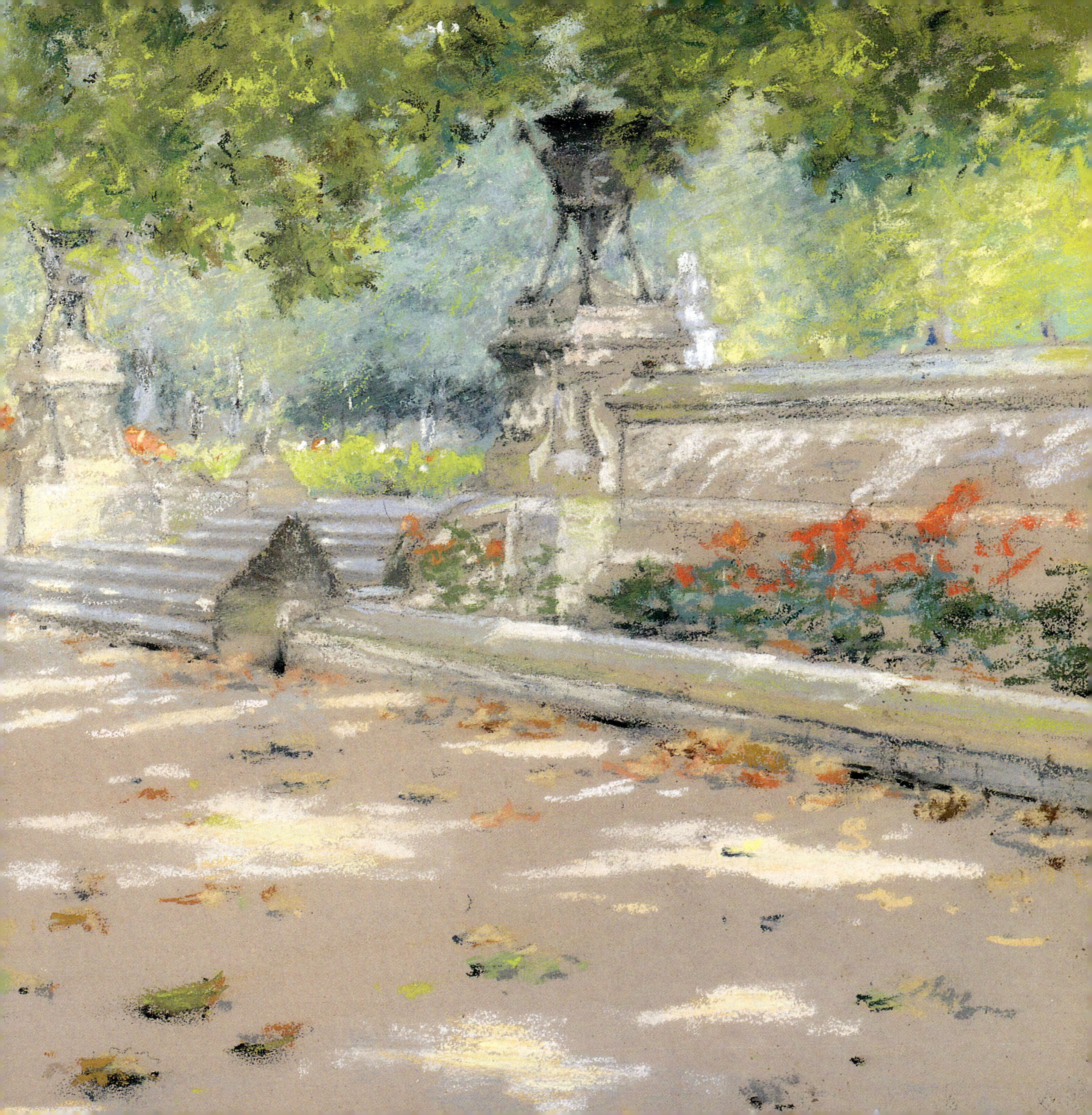

**JOHN STEUART CURRY**

1897–1946

## *Our Good Earth*

1942
watercolor
13 3/8 x 11 in.
Smithsonian American Art Museum, purchase made possible by Ralph Cross Johnson and William T. Evans

When John Steuart Curry was asked to create a monumental image for a war bond poster during World War II, he depicted a noble American farmer standing tall in his Kansas wheatfield, flanked by two carefree children. This watercolor is a study for the painting, which was then reproduced as a poster captioned "Our Good Earth—Keep It Ours."

In 1937 Curry had been hired as an artist in residence at the University of Wisconsin for the express purpose of inspiring the people of rural Wisconsin. A champion of Midwestern values and the rural lifestyle, Curry feared that war would shift the country's resources away from agriculture toward industry. He wanted to emphasize that America's farmers were making an important contribution to the war effort by raising the food needed to sustain the country's soldiers.

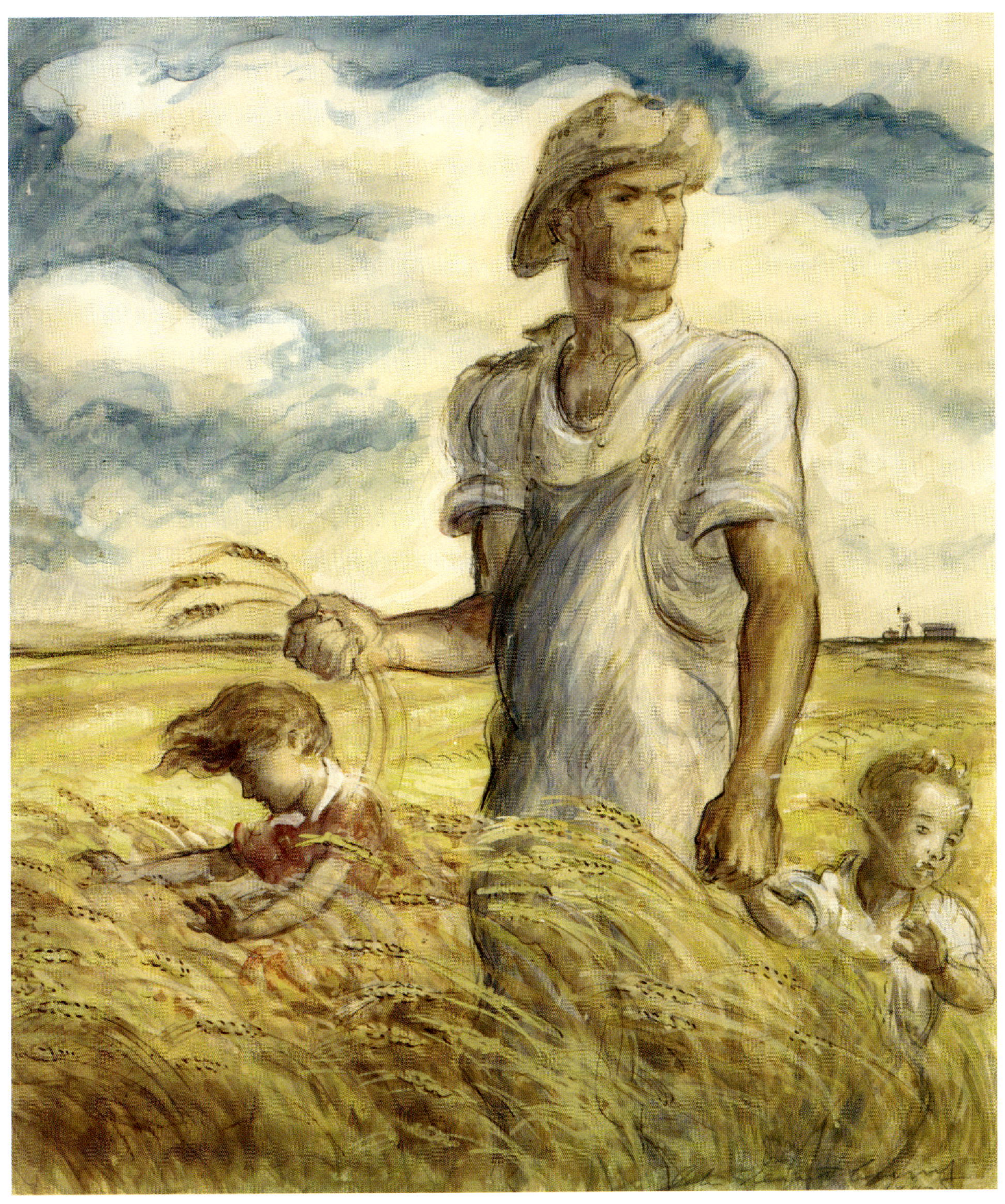

**STUART DAVIS**

1894–1964

# *Impression of the New York World's Fair*

## mural study for the Communications Building, World's Fair, Flushing, New York

1939
gouache
14 ¾ x 22 ⅛ in.
Smithsonian American Art Museum, Transfer from the United States Information Agency through the General Services Administration

Stuart Davis's *Impression of the New York World's Fair* is an especially valuable record of an important mural that no longer exists. The mural, which was created for the Communications building of the 1939 World's Fair, told the story of the "historical development of the means of communication . . . of the mechanical and electrical objectification of the human eye, ear, voice, and bodily motion." The Fair provided a much-needed vision of hope and prosperity to counteract the dislocation and confusion of the Depression. The bold, bright colors and highly abstracted forms lead the viewer's eye across the entire wall without the impediment of a single focal point. Some of the forms suggest recognizable symbols, such as trees, buildings, towers, and people, but Davis wanted the viewer to recall the mural not as "dates, costumes, materials of construction, correct historical sequence or factual information, but [as] pleasant and stimulating shape-objects in space in relation to each other."

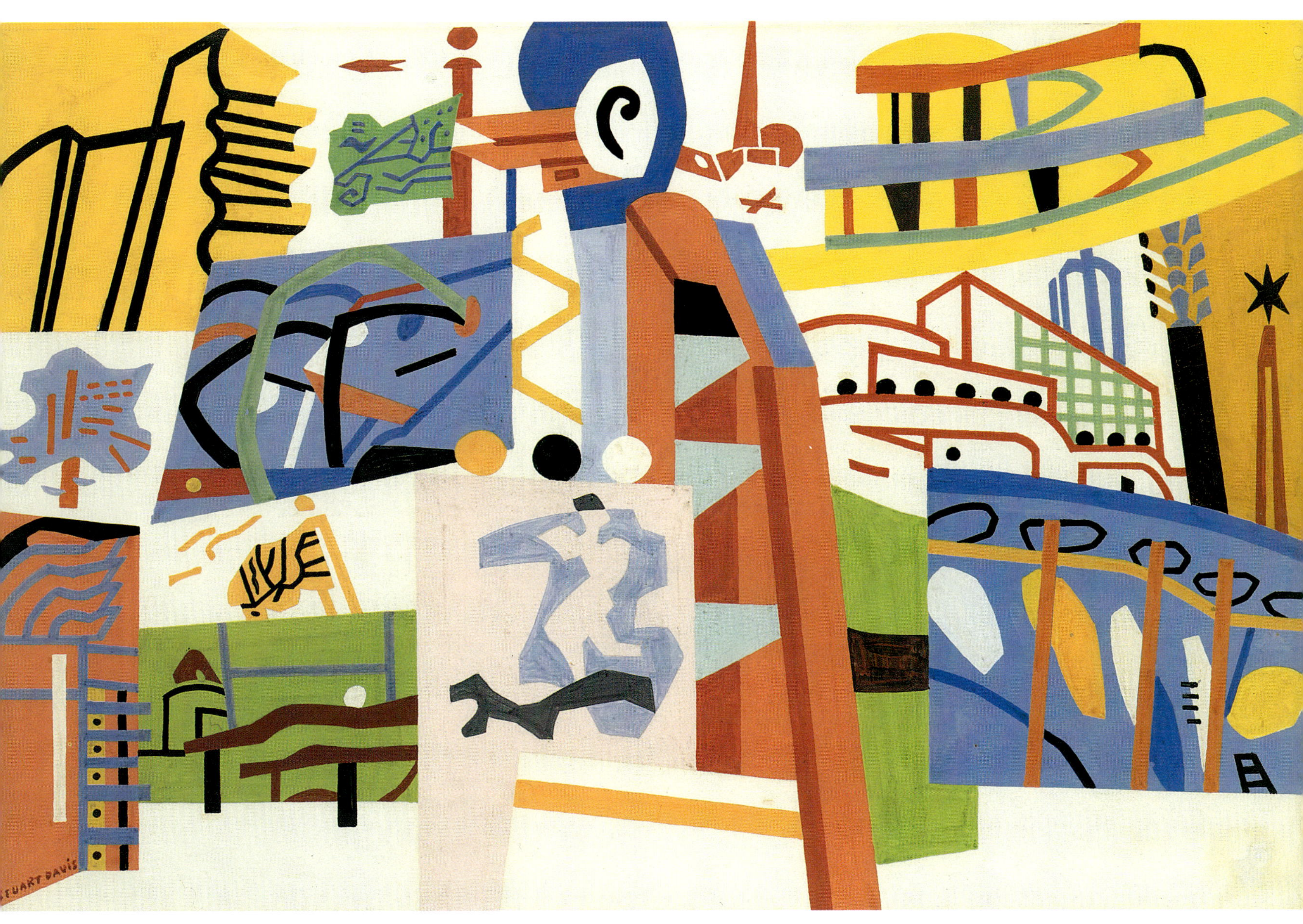
STUART DAVIS

**ROY DE FOREST**

born 1930

# *Drawing XVII*

1974
oil crayon and colored pencil
22 ½ x 30 ⅛ in.
Smithsonian American Art Museum, Gift of the Sara Roby Foundation

Unfettered imagination is at the day-glo heart of Roy De Forest's complex and whimsical compositions. "One of the most important things to me as an artist is the discovery of what is possible. . . . Drawing and even painting are much closer to the very human activity of making a mess or making mud pies than they are to learning to draw or paint. You have some color, you have some charcoal . . . what kinds of castles can you make?" Inspired by the directness and power of folk art, De Forest uses bright, primary colors, bold lines and patterns, and flat, silhouetted shapes to construct a personal fantasy. The scenery, people, and animals of his daily life in Port Costa, California, are transformed into some sort of mythological quest of man and beast.

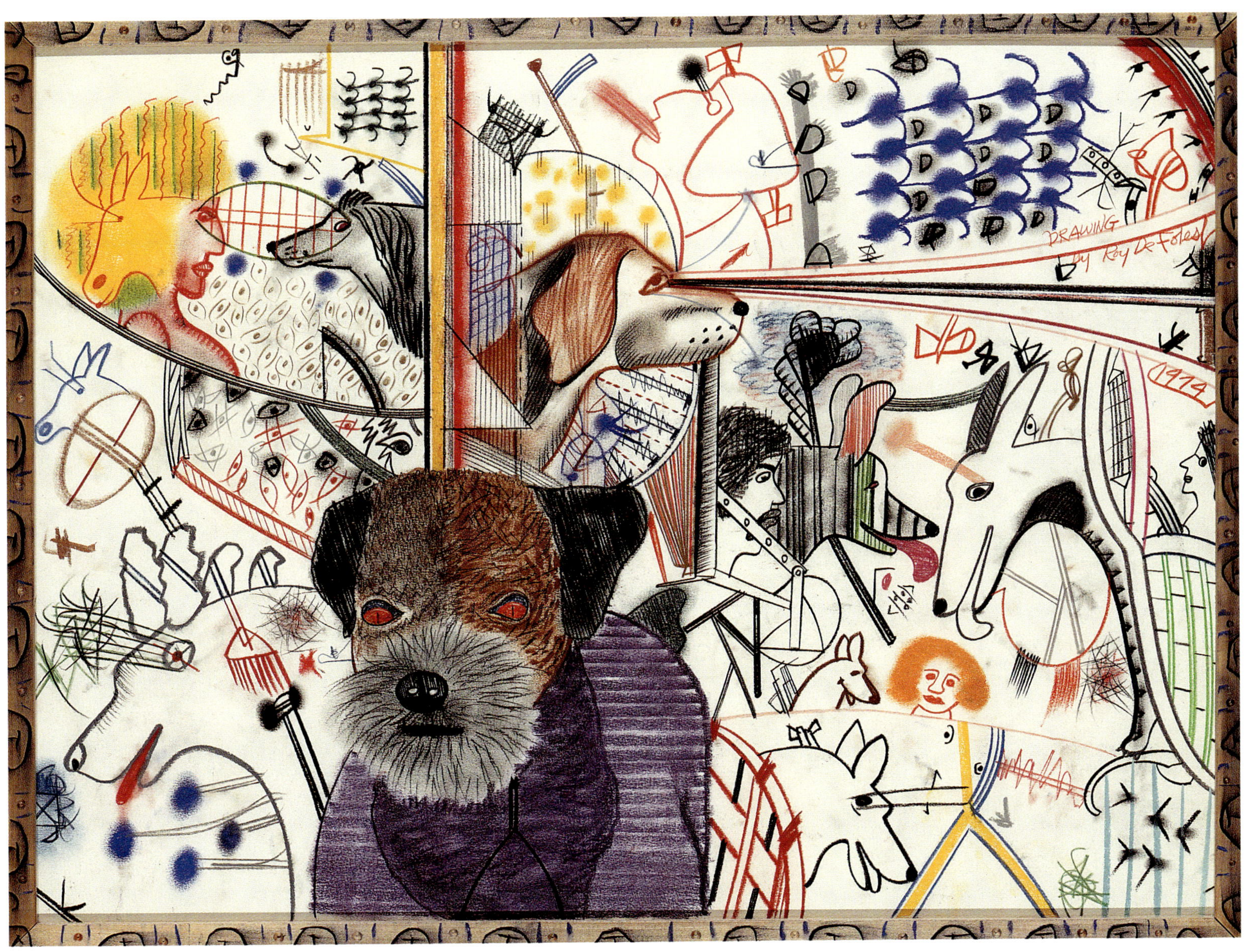
DRAWING
by Roy De Fores
1974

**WILLEM DE KOONING**

1904 Netherlands–1997 USA

## *Untitled*

1950
enamel on paper
22 x 30 in.
Smithsonian American Art Museum, purchase from the Vincent Melzac Collection through the Smithsonian Institution Collections Acquisition Program

This black-and-white drawing reveals Willem de Kooning's mastery of the spontaneous gesture in its purest form. In the service of pure abstraction, his lines move across the surface with a fluency and energy that distinguish his most accomplished work. A composition that integrates angular and curvilinear forms, this drawing captures the tension an artist experiences at the moment of creative expression.

De Kooning loved to draw. His seemingly spontaneous paintings were usually preceded by numerous drawings in which he explored ideas he would later develop on a larger scale. Yet he recognized his drawings as independent works of art, as did many other artists in his orbit, and exhibited them alongside his paintings throughout his career.

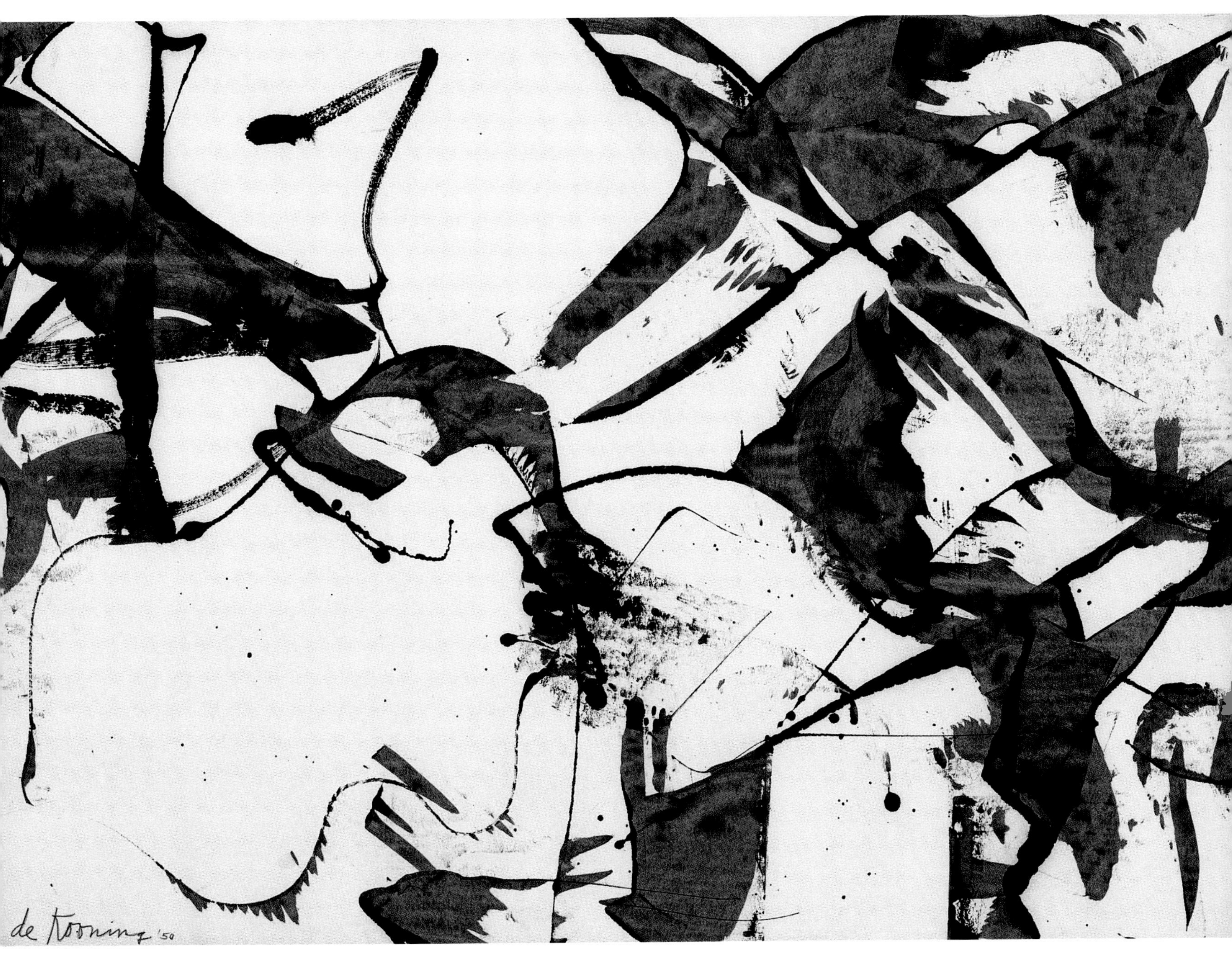
de Kooning '50

**DOROTHY DEHNER**

1901–1994

## *The People in the Story; Bolton Landing*

1949
pen and ink and watercolor wash
18 1/8 x 22 7/8 in.
Smithsonian American Art Museum

*The People in the Story; Bolton Landing* refers to the artist's life at Bolton Landing in upstate New York during the 1930s and '40s. During the time she was married to the sculptor David Smith, whose career overshadowed her own, Dehner was left to care for the farm while Smith focused on his art. She produced few works but developed a personal iconography of abstract forms that first appeared in her drawings and paintings, and ultimately in her sculpture. Though the title of this drawing suggests that specific people are represented, the forms relate instead to the natural world with only occasional reference to human beings. The tall, vertical forms evoke totemic presences, but the variations from one to the next endow each form with an individual personality.

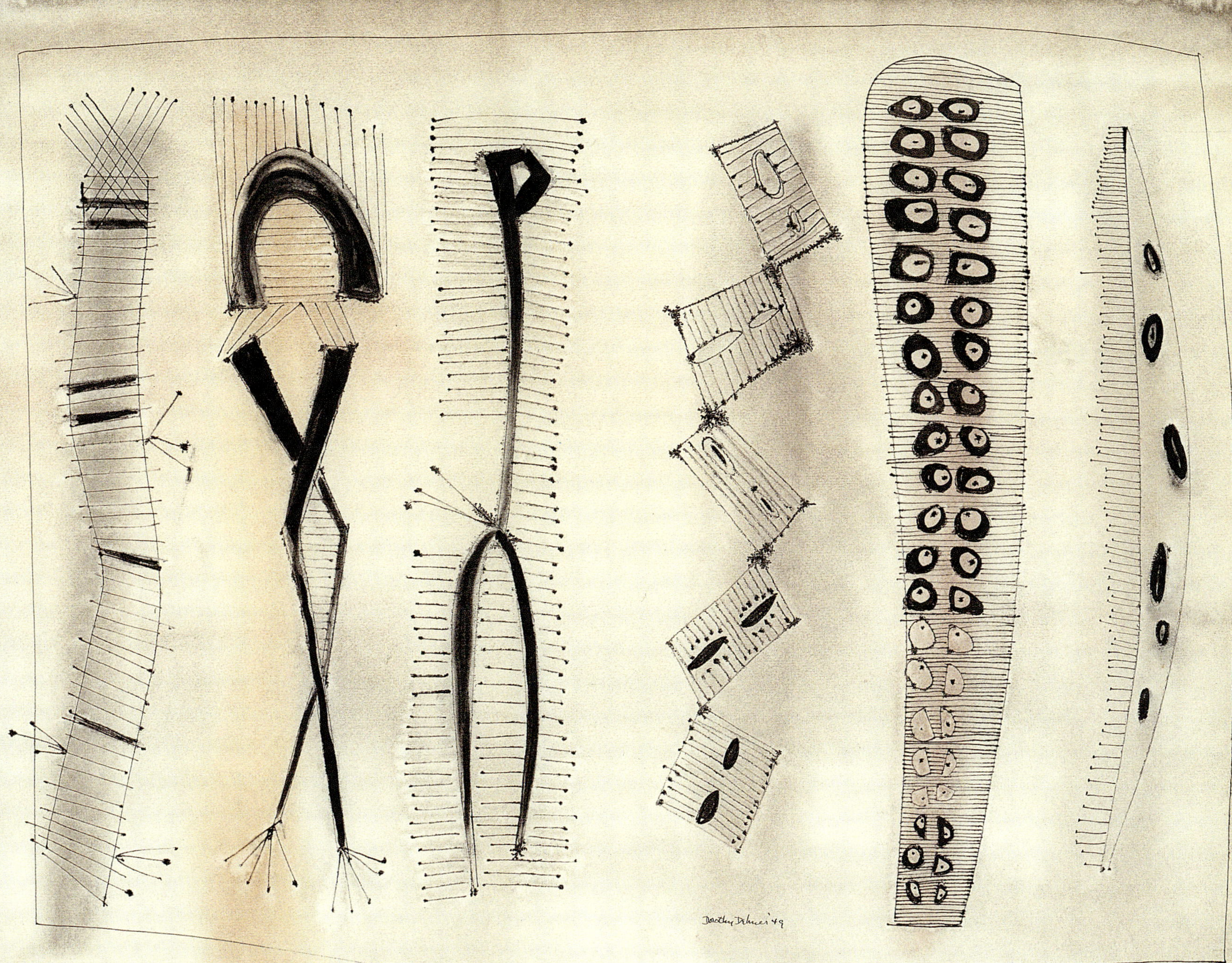

**THOMAS WILMER DEWING**

1851–1938

## *Walt Whitman*

1875
chalk
24 ½ x 18 in.
Smithsonian American Art Museum, purchase through the Robert Tyler Davis Memorial Fund

Whether Dewing drew this portrait from life or from a photograph of the poet is not known, but its resemblance to several photographs suggests the latter. By 1875, Whitman had suffered a paralytic stroke, and his health was in decline, but his reputation as one of America's greatest living poets had been firmly established. Dewing expressed his admiration for Whitman by idealizing his image. He gave the poet's full beard a silky quality, and he reduced the wrinkles of his face and eyelids to create a monumental and eternal presence.

The artist began his drawing with faint pencil lines, and proceeded to model the features with delicate, cross-hatched chalk lines, which he then "smudged and smoothed" so that the individual lines seem to disappear. Highlights of white chalk throughout the face enliven the image. When this drawing was exhibited in Boston in 1875, critics singled it out for its excellent technique.

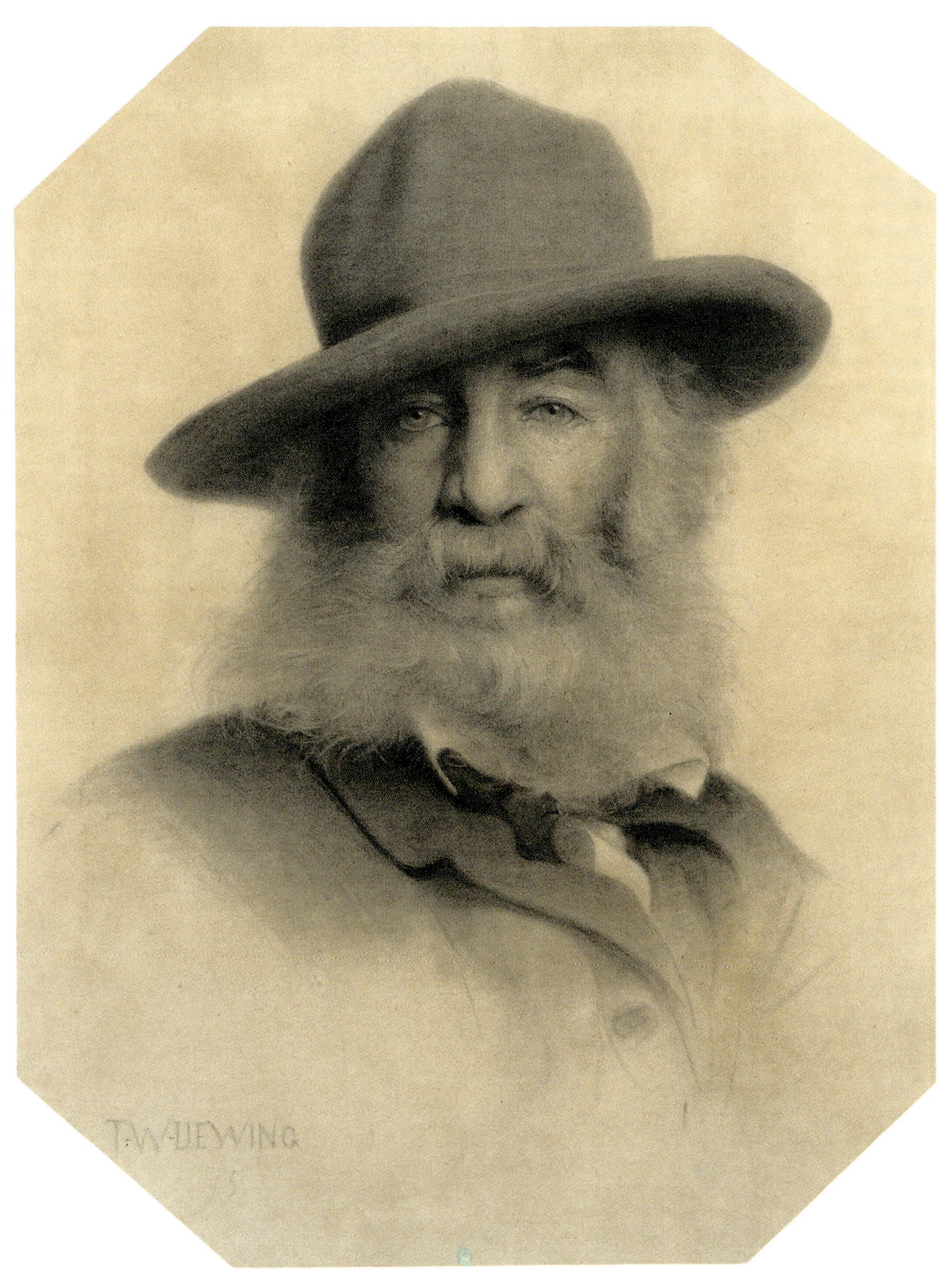
T.W. DEWING

**APRIL GORNIK**

born 1953

## *Storm and Fires*

1990
charcoal and pastel
$47\ 1/8 \times 38\ 1/4$ in.
Smithsonian American Art Museum, purchase through the friends of Philip Desind

Clouds and smoke swirl across the paper, drawing us into the ominous power and sense of mystery inherent in *Storm and Fires.* The drawing expresses the thrill Gornik finds in the path of an approaching storm. She has remarked of similar works, "I love imminent storms—the charge in the air is incredibly exciting just before a storm erupts."

Inspired by dreams and recollections rather than specific landscapes, Gornik draws artifical environments. Her images are deeply personal responses to a melange of experiences. She has become well known for her evocative vistas devoid of human presence that simultaneously attract and repel the viewer. "My work is about the underbelly of the beauty of nature, and the dark side of nature is its indifference. Nature isn't friendly, nor is it unfriendly—it's the perfect embodiment of the Other."

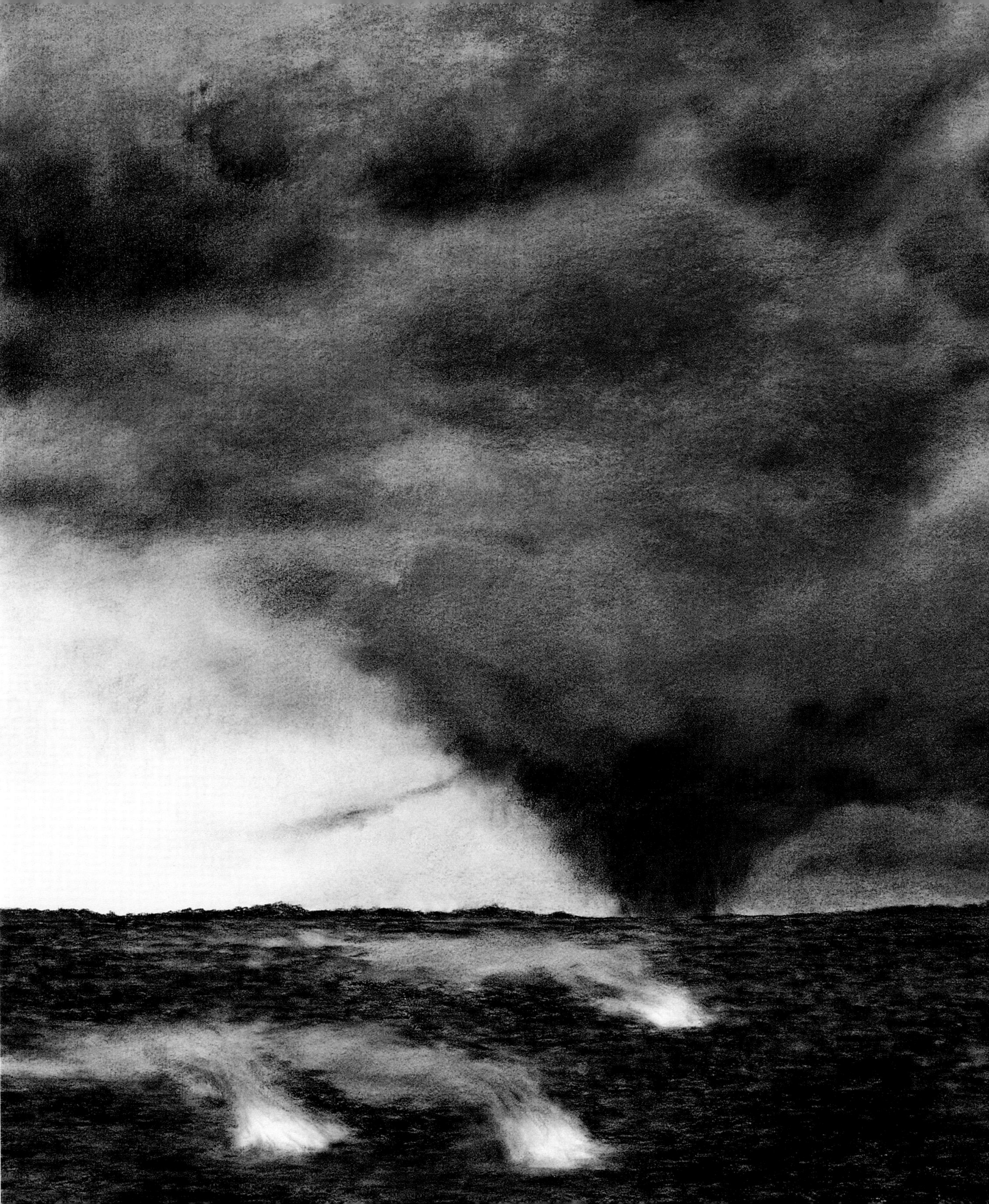

**MORRIS GRAVES**

1910–2001

# *Folded Wings—Memory—& the Moon Weeping*

about 1942–43
ink wash and gouache
29 3/8 x 23 3/4 in.
Smithsonian American Art Museum, Gift of Michael and Caryl Marsh

*Folded Wings—Memory—& the Moon Weeping* combines several of Morris Graves's most important themes in a single, poetic image. As a master of contemplative, spiritual expression, Graves used natural forms to symbolize his state of mind and inner vision. For Graves, his art was a means to reach a higher stage of consciousness. His image of a bird with folded wings and the moon seem to emerge from his transcendent imagination, the artist's "inner eye," rather than from direct observation. They take form not only as personal memories, but also as a collective memory that persists through time, across cultures. The transparent, abstract forms suggest an image engraved in the face of a rock, worn away by time and weather, at once fading and accumulating new meaning.

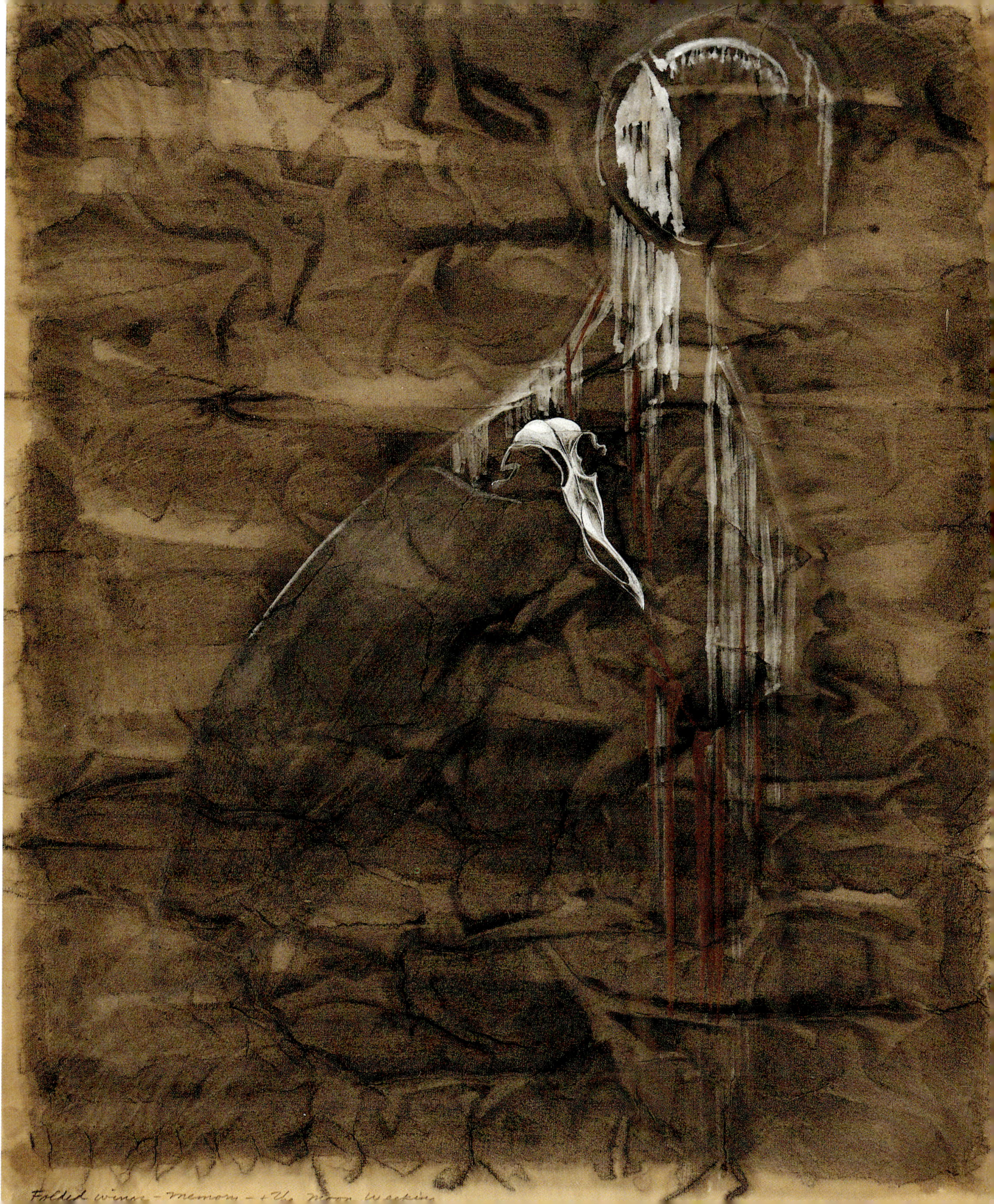
Folded wings - Memory - + the Moon

**PHILIP GUSTON**

1913 Canada–1980 USA

## *Hovering*

1976
ink
18 1/4 x 24 1/8 in.
Smithsonian American Art Museum, Gift of Ruth and Jacob Kainen

During the 1970s Philip Guston shocked the New York art world when he exhibited figurative paintings that turned away from the abstract expressionist style for which he had become recognized. Reacting against the "purity" of abstraction, he sought to express his anxieties about the violence, assassinations, and political cynicism that surrounded him. In both his paintings and drawings, he created a vocabulary of bold lines, cartoon-like forms, and subjective symbolism to visualize his thoughts on a range of personal, social, and philosophical issues.

In *Hovering* the artist seems to be contemplating the nature of creativity, its sources, pitfalls, contradictions, and endurance. The large, bulbous head is Guston, the artist, while the faceless, vertical head at his side is his wife, Musa, literally his muse. The clock with numbers refers to the passage of time, while the watch face without numbers suggests immortality. Guston juxtaposes comic, grotesque, and serious elements as a means of pondering the ironies and ambiguities of questions that have no simple answers.

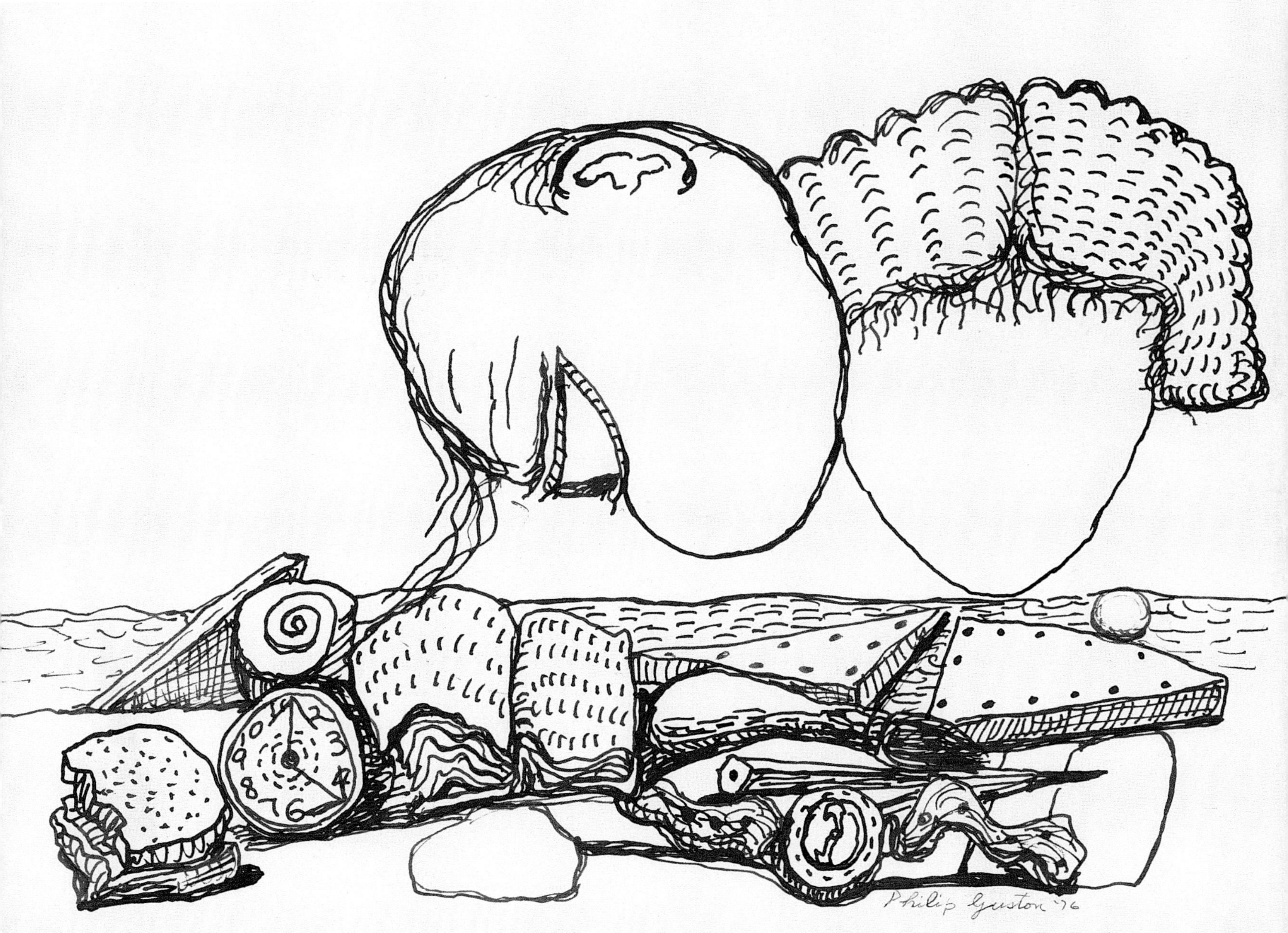
Philip Guston '76

**CHILDE HASSAM**

1859–1935

## *Lillie (Lillie Langtry)*

about 1898
watercolor and gouache
24 ¼ x 19 ¾ in.
Smithsonian American Art Museum, Gift of John Gellatly

Lillie Langtry was an English actress, famous as one of the country's most beautiful women. Her American tour, spanning five consecutive years, was a grand success, with a town in Texas named in her honor by Justice of the Peace Roy Bean. In 1898, during this tour, Lillie posed for Childe Hassam in his Fifth Avenue studio. Hassam recalled "having been introduced to her by Stanford White, the great friend of not only all the painters, but of all the good-looking women."

She was about to marry Sir Hugo de Bathe at the time she posed, and she asked the artist not to use her full name when he exhibited the portrait. Shortly after it was completed, the artist exhibited the watercolor at the American Water Color Society exhibition with the title *Lillie.*

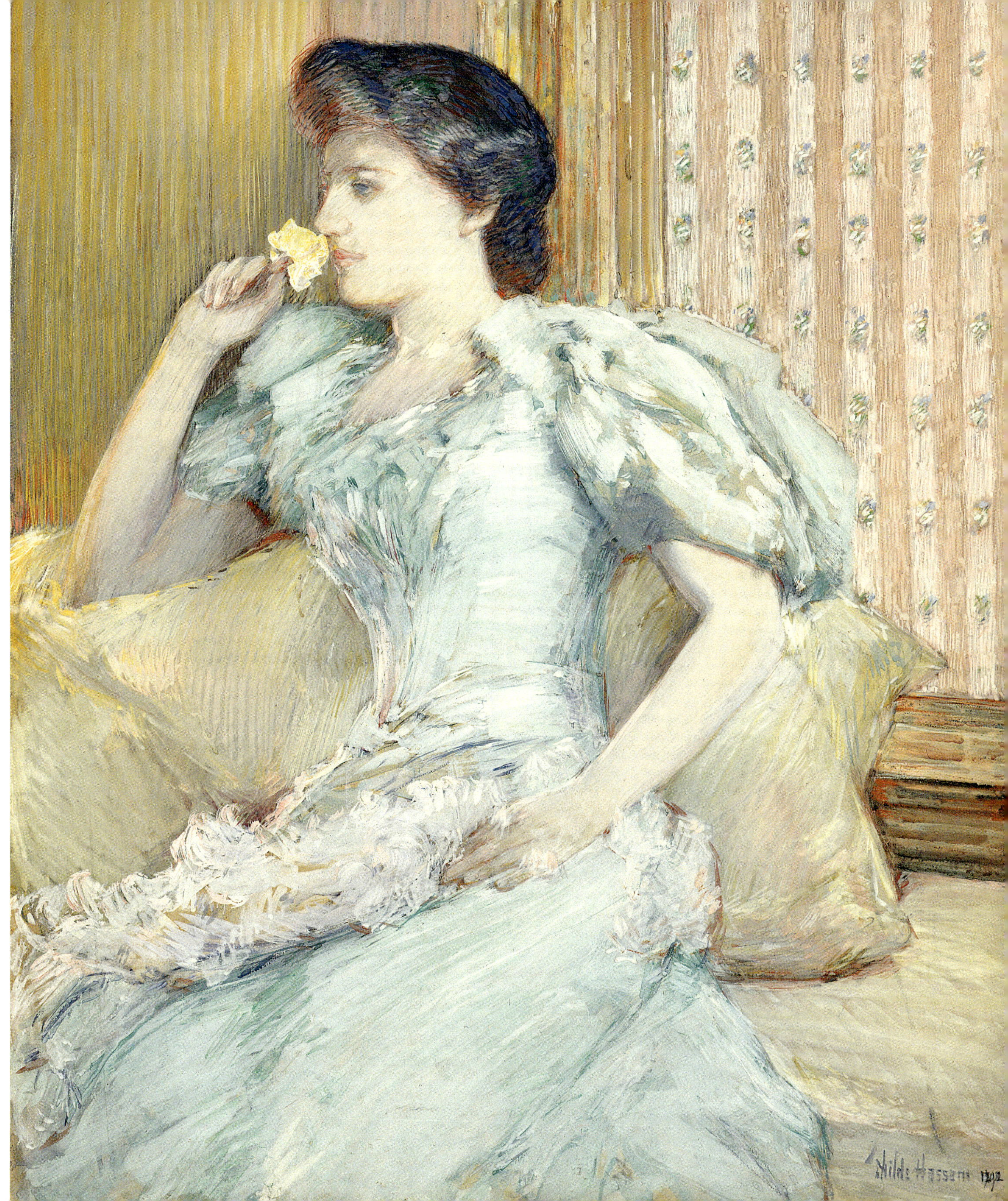
Childe Hassam

**CHILDE HASSAM**

1859–1935

## *Thaxter's Garden*

1892
watercolor
19 7/8 x 14 1/8 in.
Smithsonian American Art Museum, Gift of John Gellatly

Celia Thaxter's home on Appledore, one of the Isles of Shoals off the coast of New Hampshire, was celebrated for its luxuriant flower garden, full of brilliant color and wild beauty. Childe Hassam belonged to a circle of artists and writers who gathered at the informal salon she hosted during summers on the island. A poet and journalist, Thaxter published *An Island Garden,* for which Hassam drew illustrations. The book appeared in 1894, the year of Thaxter's death.

The clear light, fresh sea air, and jewel-like colors of his friend's garden energized Hassam. He painted some of his freest, most experimental compositions here, and he continued to return to the site for years after Thaxter's death. By far, of all the sites Hassam painted, the Isles of Shoals constitutes the majority. Some of his most successful paintings and watercolors depict her home, her garden, and views from the island.

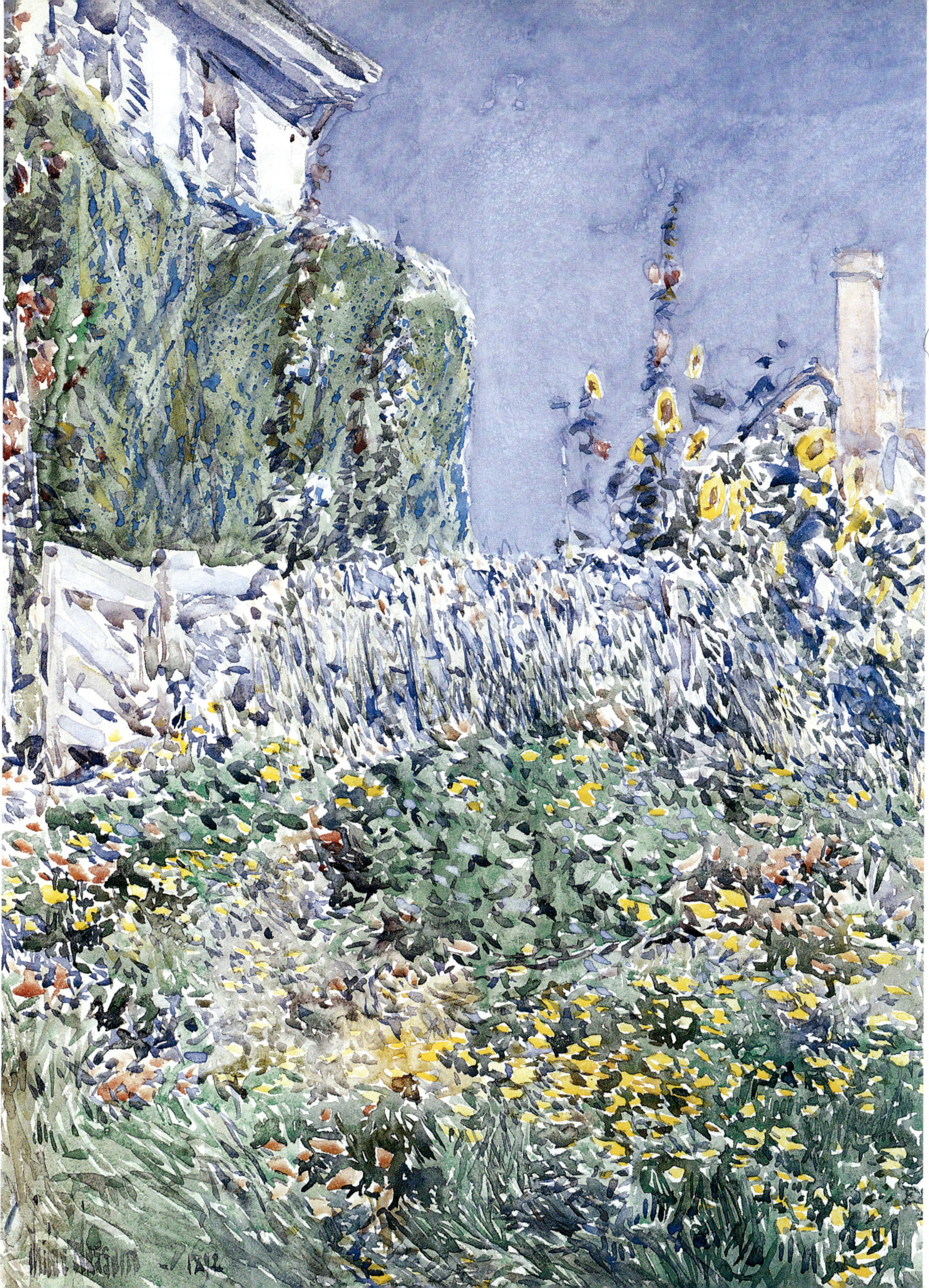

**WINSLOW HOMER**
1836–1910

## *Bear Hunting, Prospect Rock*

1892
watercolor and pencil
13 7/8 x 20 1/8 in.
Smithsonian American Art Museum, Gift of John Gellatly

Guns ready, two grizzled hunters balance against a steep rock face that drops precipitously to a valley floor far below. Though no bear appears in the painting, the danger is palpable. The figures in this work are modeled on guides from the North Woods Club where Homer spent much of his time. Prospect Rock, located less than a quarter of a mile away from the clubhouse and reached by a graded trail, was one of Homer's favorite spots to paint. He often rearranged or modified details of the landscape to suit the needs of his composition. In this watercolor Homer presents man as an essential part of nature, neither overwhelmed by its grandeur, nor fully in control of the wilderness.

Winslow Homer began painting Adirondack subjects in 1870, the year of his first visit to the region in upstate New York, and returned to them intermittently over four decades. While other artists who depicted trappers, hunters, and woodsmen in the mountains emphasized the strong verticals and diagonals that typify mountain scenery, Homer drew attention to the figures as the most important vertical elements in otherwise horizontal compositions.

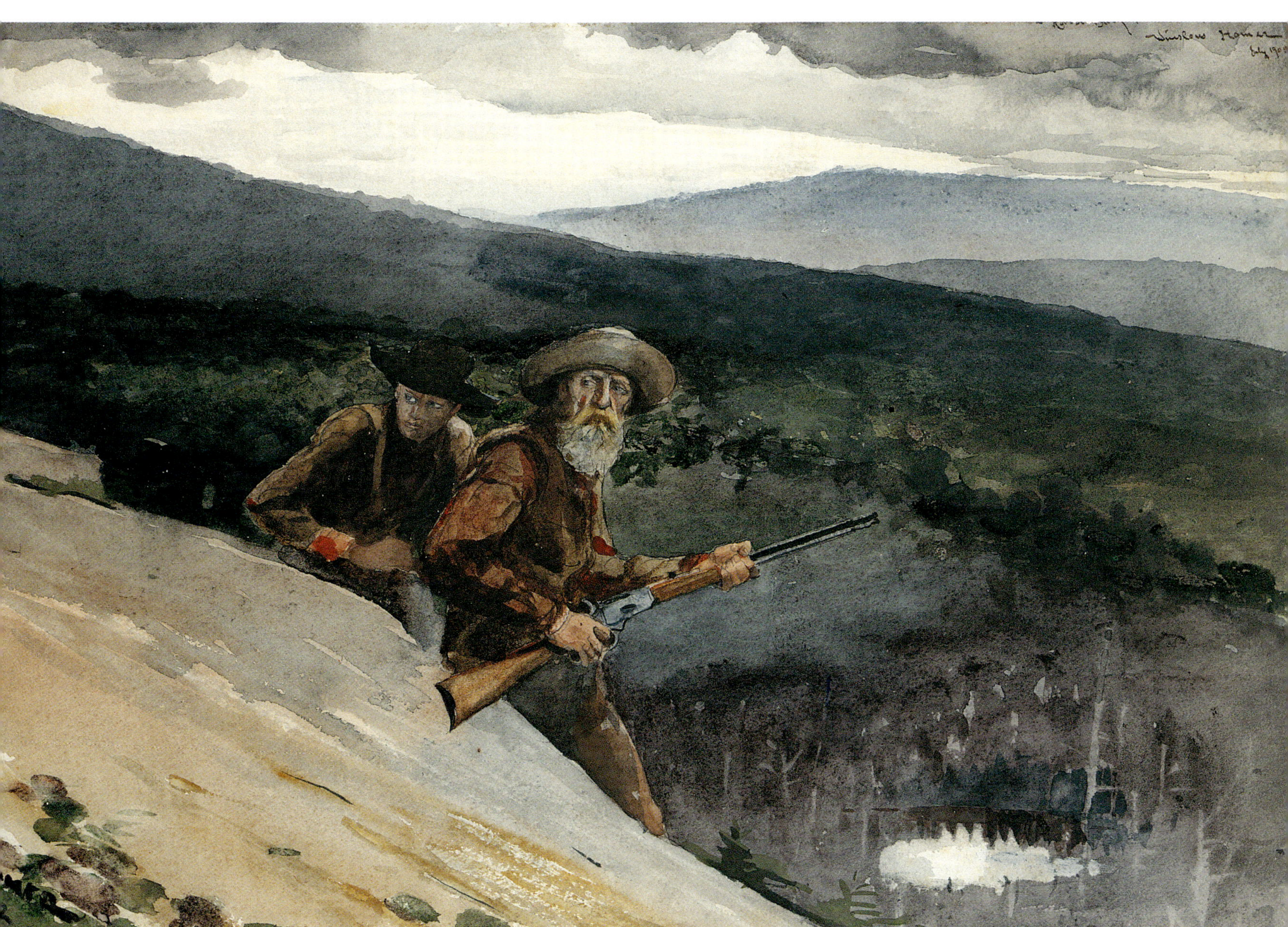
Winslow Homer

**EDWARD HOPPER**

1882–1967

## *White River at Sharon*

1937
watercolor and pencil
21 3/4 x 29 3/4 in.
Smithsonian American Art Museum, Gift of the Sara Roby Foundation

*White River at Sharon* shows Edward Hopper working in the free, spontaneous style that characterizes his finest watercolors. Hopper painted his rural landscape watercolors during summers spent wandering through New England and Cape Cod in his periodic search for new ideas for paintings. This scene was painted in September 1937, when he and his wife were visiting the farm of friends in Vermont. He captured the distinctive light of early autumn in a landscape seemingly devoid of man's presence. Careful examination of the scene, however, reveals a road barely visible in the center of the composition as well as a railroad embankment in the upper right, behind the dying tree.

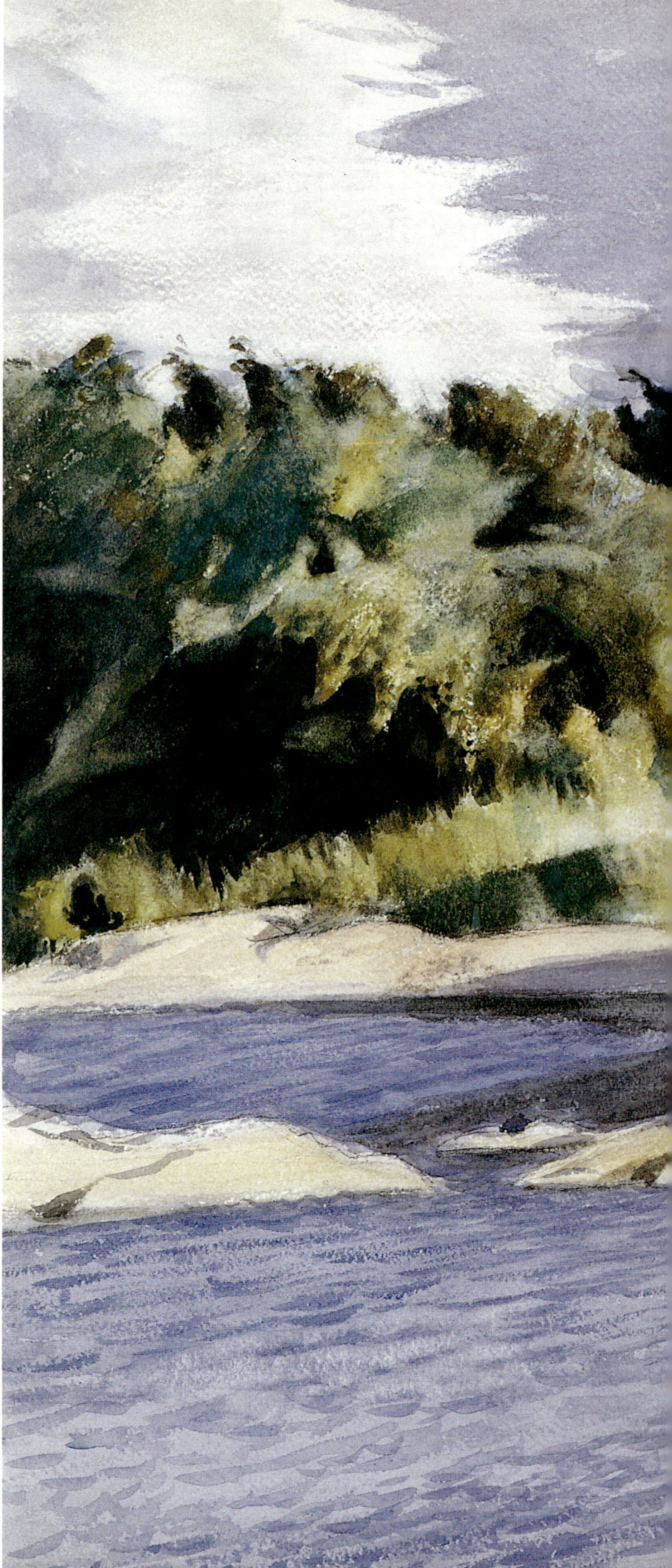

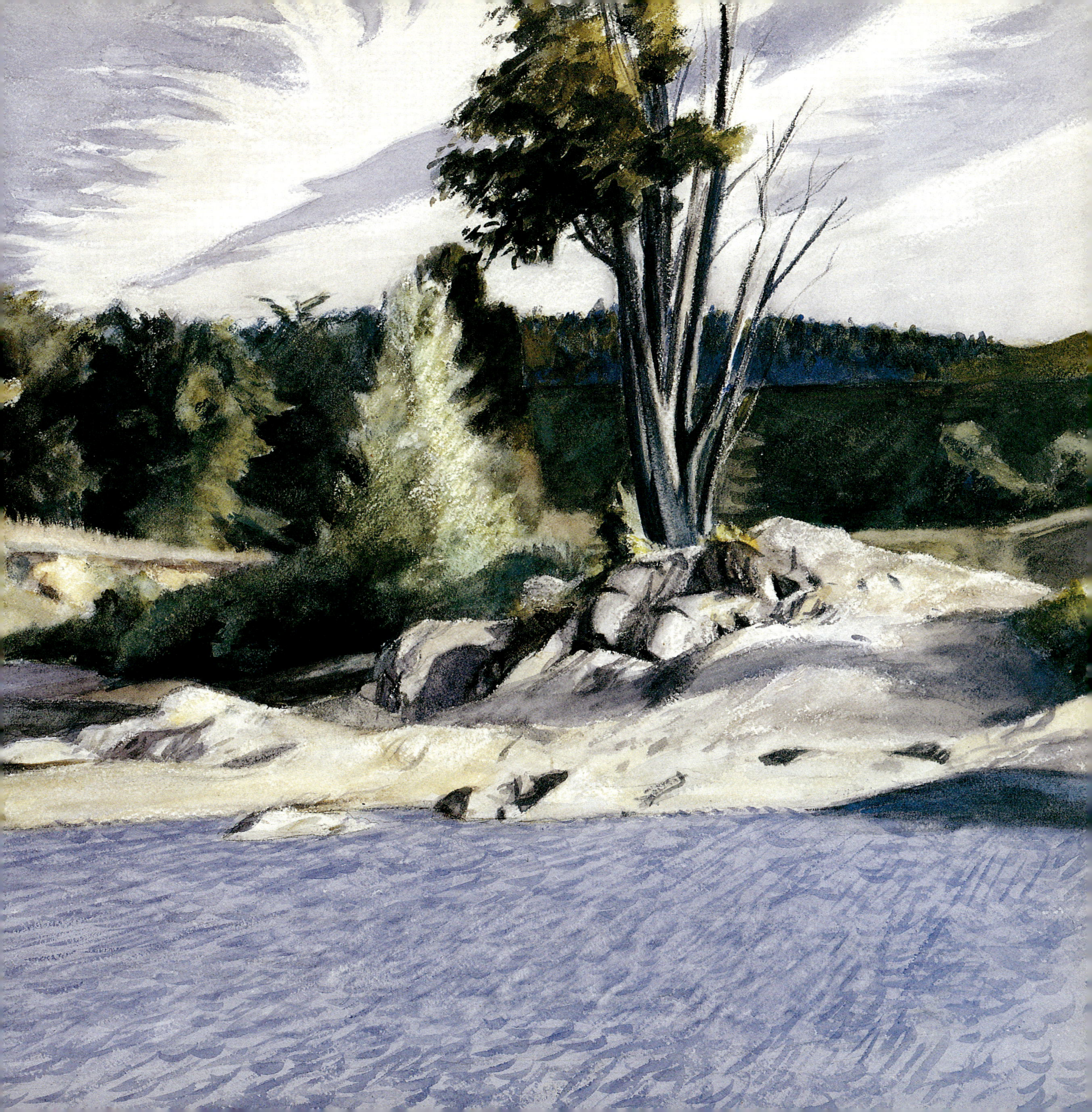

**BILL JENSEN**

born 1945

## *Drawing for Legion*

1983–84
charcoal
21 ¾ x 18 in.
Smithsonian American Art Museum, purchase made possible by J.R. Hodge, The National Institute Gift, B.C. Reynolds, S.I. Transfers and Catherine Wiley

Working in a relatively small format, Bill Jensen's drawings, watercolors, and paintings combine an intimacy of scale with an intensity of expression. His dense, compact, and heavily worked forms strain the boundaries of his composition with an energy generated from within. In *Drawing for Legion,* religious and sexual allusions, such as the trumpet-like forms and phallic shapes, suggest both physical and spiritual redemption on the Day of Judgment.

Drawing is an essential step in the creative process for Jensen. Beginning with small sketches of objects he encounters in the course of his daily life, which often reappear as details of paintings, he proceeds to charcoal drawings in which he defines the forms, composition, and expressive dynamics that usually change little from this stage to the final painting. The next step is usually a watercolor version where he establishes color relationships. In the painted version of the theme, he concentrates on the patchy, roughed-up, rubbed-down, layered and incised surfaces.

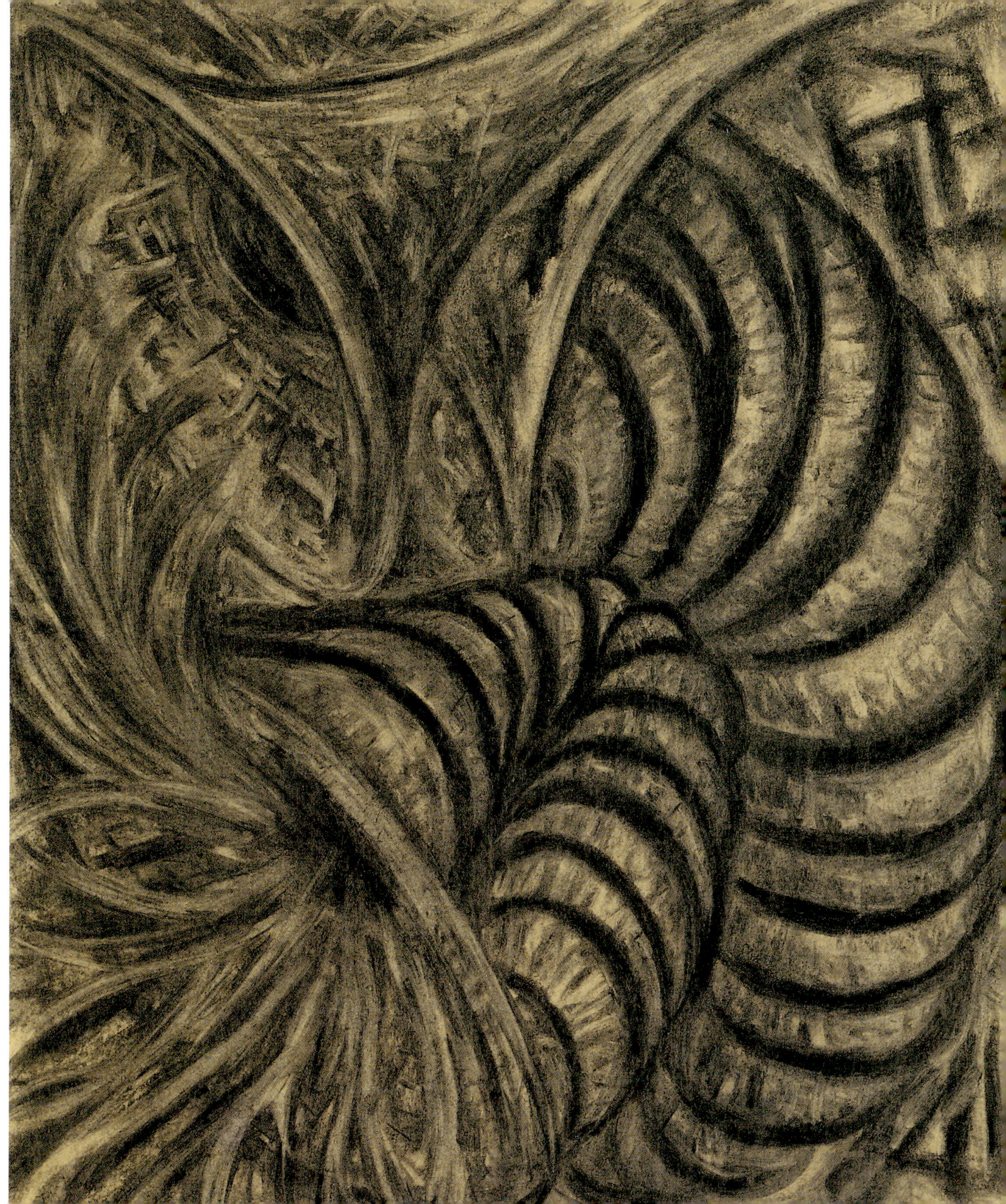

**LUIS JIMENEZ**

born 1940

## *Coyote*

1993
watercolor with pencil
48 x 52 in.
Smithsonian American Art Museum, Gift of Frank K. Ribelin

This image of a dead coyote is an especially poignant one for Luis Jimenez. Until recently, coyotes were killed by bounty hunters and their skins were strung along fences marking the U.S.-Mexican border. Although this practice is no longer common, trappers throughout the West still hunt coyotes. Jimenez appears to sympathize with the animals as prey rather than fearing them as predators. At the time he created this watercolor, the artist was facing the loss of sight in one of his eyes, and he strongly identified with the trapped and threatened animals.

In addition to his empathy for the fate of coyotes, Jimenez recognizes their importance in the folklore of his native Southwest. Coyote, the trickster of Native American storytellers, represents cunning and intelligence. Along the border, labor and drug traffickers are called coyotes, as are people of mixed Anglo and Hispanic or Native American blood. A dead coyote implies an attack on these traditions as much as on the animal itself.

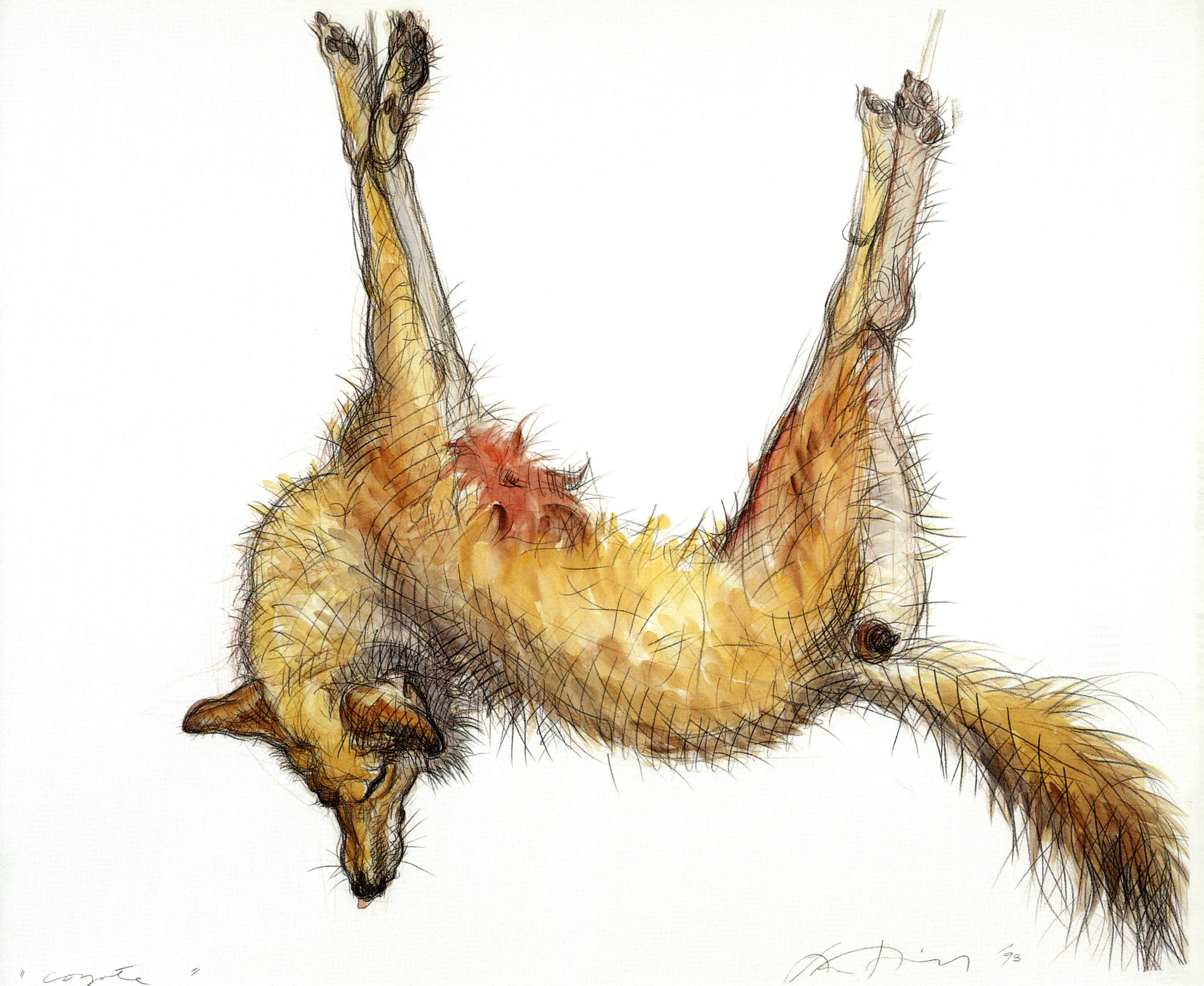
'coyote'

**WILLIAM H. JOHNSON**

1901–1970

## *Going Out*

about 1939–42
gouache,
pen and ink,
and pencil
15 x 11 3/8 in.
Smithsonian
American Art
Museum, Gift of
the Harmon
Foundation

A mother and daughter, dressed to the nines, are ready for a night on the town. The mother has chosen a bright red beret to match her lipstick, and put on her best high-heeled shoes. The daughter has topped her carefully coiffed hair with a jaunty bow, and carries two abstracted flowers. Johnson reveals a sense of humor in the flower forms that also suggest two lollipops and two breasts.

The charming naiveté of William H. Johnson's *Going Out* reveals his delight in rediscovering black culture upon his return to New York after spending many years in Scandanavia. Determined to paint his own people in the rich variety of their daily activities, Johnson had many opportunities to observe members of the black community in Harlem, where he taught painting at the Harlem Community Art Center.

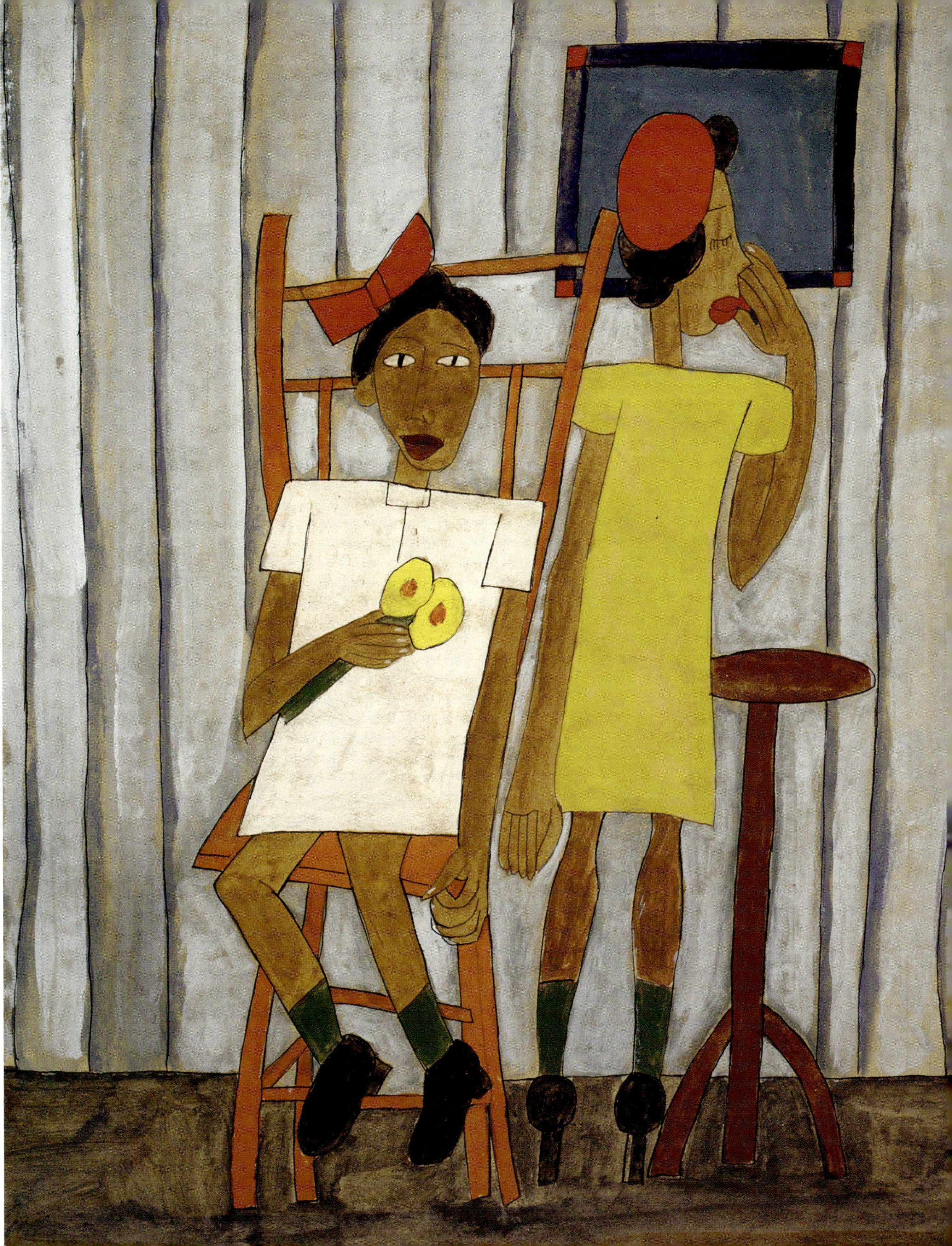

**WILLIAM H. JOHNSON**

1901–1970

## *Lunchtime Rest*

about 1940–41
tempera and pen and ink
13 ³⁄₈ x 18 in.
Smithsonian American Art Museum, Gift of the Harmon Foundation

The brilliant colors and bold stripes of this composition recall the multi-stripe designs of West African textiles, while the patterns of distinct areas of land suggest the pieced, freehand quilt-work of the African American tradition. Striking color relationships and strong rhythmic patterns distinguish Johnson's scenes of rural life, revealing his sophisticated understanding of both the folk art tradition and contemporary modernist abstraction.

William H. Johnson pursued themes relating to his own heritage in the rural South in scenes such as *Lunch Time Rest.* He had not visited the South for many years, so he based his pictures on memories and his vivid imagination. He focused on rural workers' mundane activities, such as picking crops, drawing well water, or operating farm machinery, to emphasize the dignity of their work without romanticizing it.

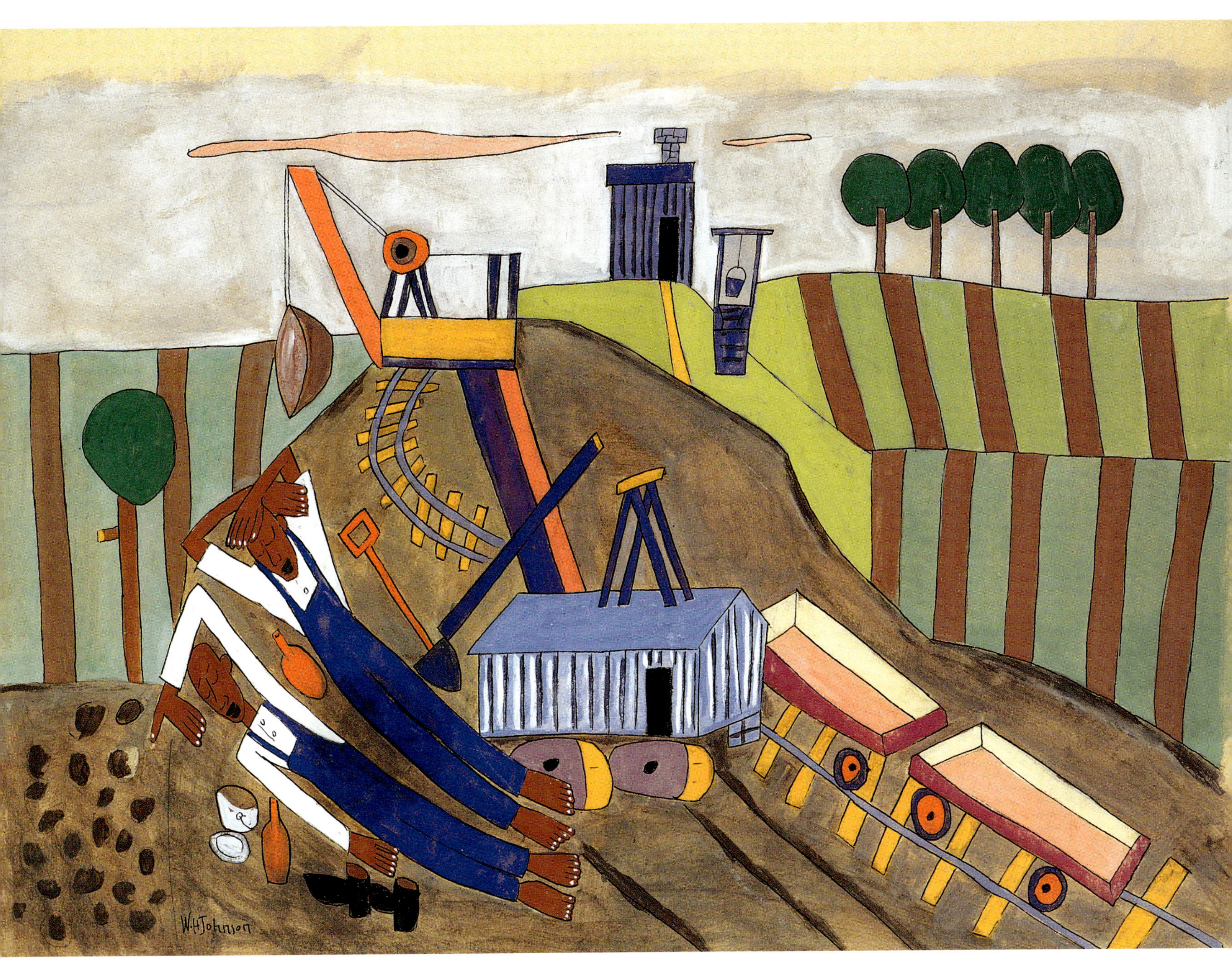
W.H.Johnson

**JOHN FREDERICK KENSETT**

1816–1872

## *Standing Artist*

about 1845–47
pencil and watercolor
11 1/4 x 8 5/8 in.
Smithsonian American Art Museum

This engaging portrait of a young artist with his art materials strapped to his back recalls the two summers in the mid-1840s when John Frederick Kensett, one of the leading painters of the Hudson River School, made walking tours of the Italian countryside. Dressed in sturdy shoes, leggings, and hat, the artist is well prepared for hiking. His knapsack, sketch umbrella, sketchbook, and mahlstick, which seems to double as a walking stick, show that he is prepared to work outdoors. The figure may be Kensett himself, or one of his colleagues on the European sojourn such as Benjamin Champney, but the details are so generalized that it is difficult to identify the specific model. Watercolors have always been especially popular with artists who draw outdoors, because they are light, portable, fast-drying, and excellent for capturing fleeting effects of light and color.

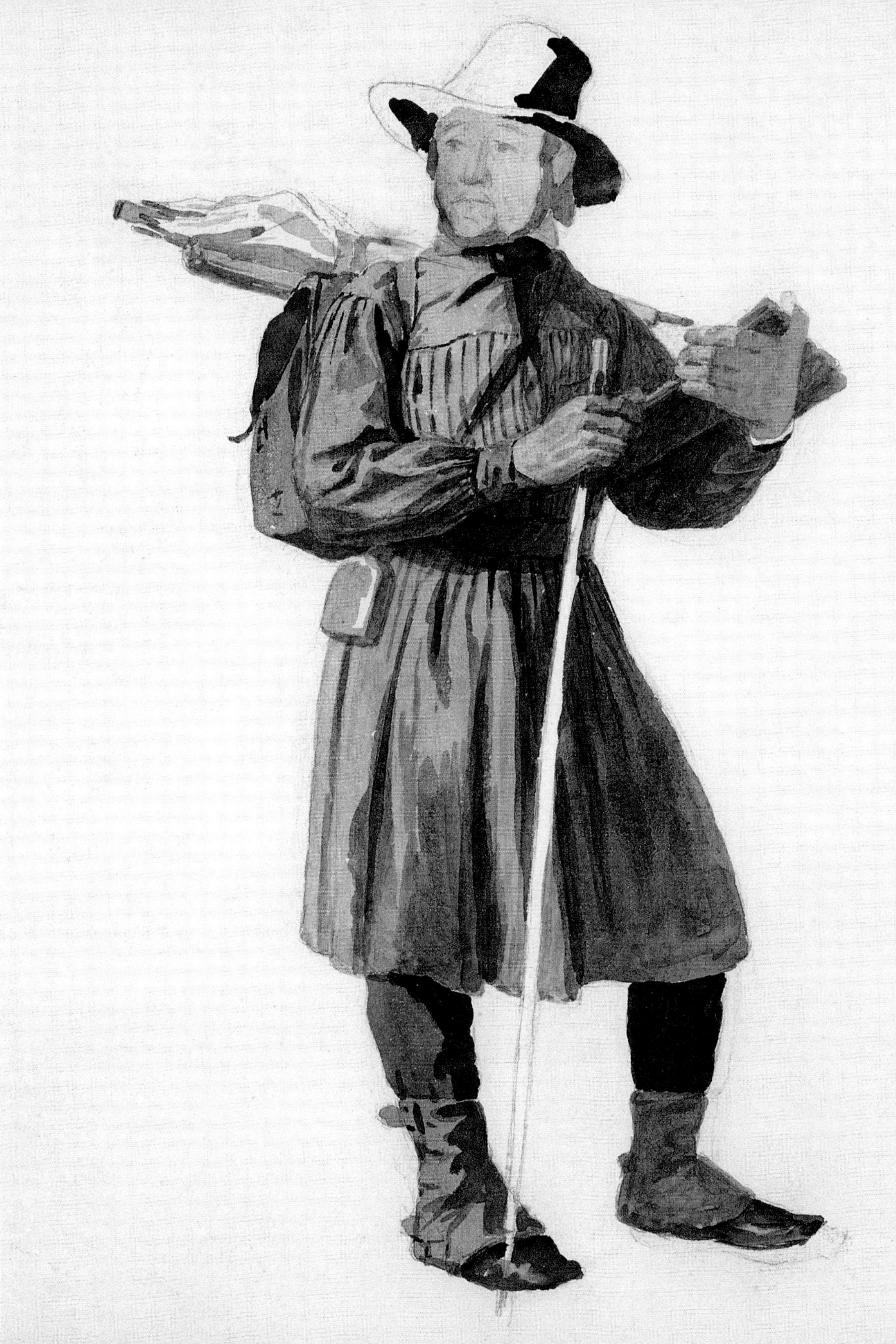

**JOHN LA FARGE**

1835–1910

## *Water Lily in Sunlight*

about 1883
watercolor
8 1/4 x 8 1/4 in.
Smithsonian American Art Museum, Gift of John Gellatly

Despite its modest size, *Water Lily in Sunlight* summarizes the full range of John La Farge's interests at the height of his career. This sensuous and decorative image epitomizes the suggestive naturalism by which he transformed accurate depictions of nature into poetic visions. La Farge took advantage of the ease and fluidity of the watercolor medium to loosen his brushstrokes and suggest, rather than describe, the subtleties of nature. The artful asymmetry of the composition recalls his interest in Japanese design, as does the bird's-eye perspective on his subject. The translucent colors and concern for light extend interests that he had begun to explore in his stained glass window designs for private homes. The contrasting densities of pigment reveal his mastery of the watercolor technique and suggest the pleasure he took in the physical properties of the medium. Shortly after this work was completed, a critic remarked: "It is on these modest water-colors that his fame, in the future, promises to rest."

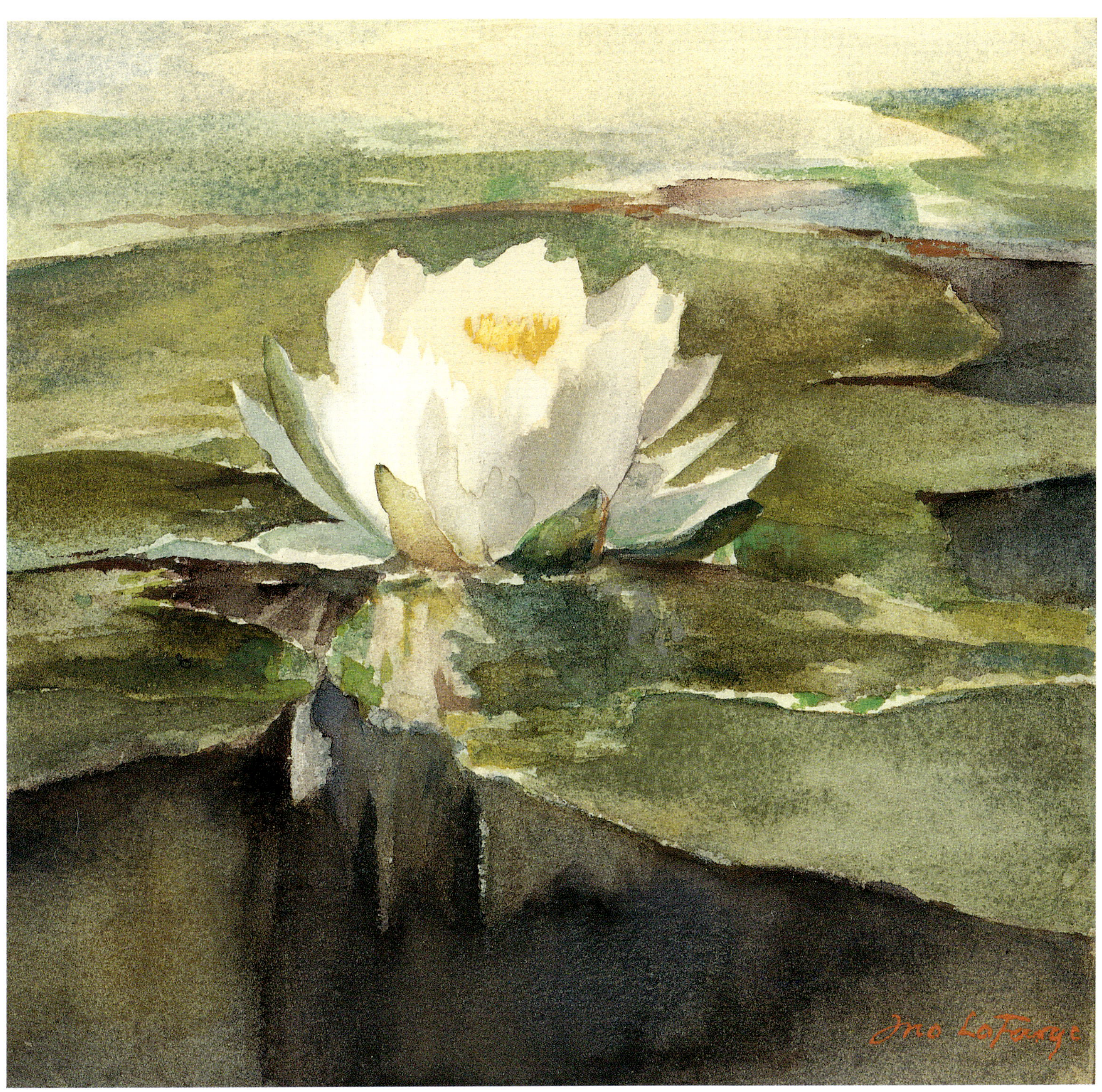
Jno LaFarge

**LOUIS LOZOWICK**

1892 Russia–1973 USA

## *Stage Setting for* "Gas"

1926
ink, tempera, and pencil
19 3/8 x 12 3/8 in.
Smithsonian American Art Museum

Lozowick had seen a production of *Gas,* Georg Kaiser's expressionist, World War I drama, in Berlin. The play's main character is an Everyman who tries to convince workers to rebel against their meaningless jobs at a plant producing poison gas. When the director of a New York production of this play learned of the artist's interest in machine imagery, he commissioned Lozowick to design the stage set. While the stark, black lines and shapes suggest metallic machinery, the actual set was built of wood and did not live up to the sleekness of form the artist envisioned in this sketch.

Lozowick explained his design: "The platforms, levels, stairs, towers arranged horizontally, vertically, and at diagonals allow an effective distribution of groups and afford the actors a possibility of free movement, up, down, forward, backward, in several directions, without impeding the action of others; to accomplish, in brief, the maximum of action in the minimum of space, being at the same time in full view of the audience."

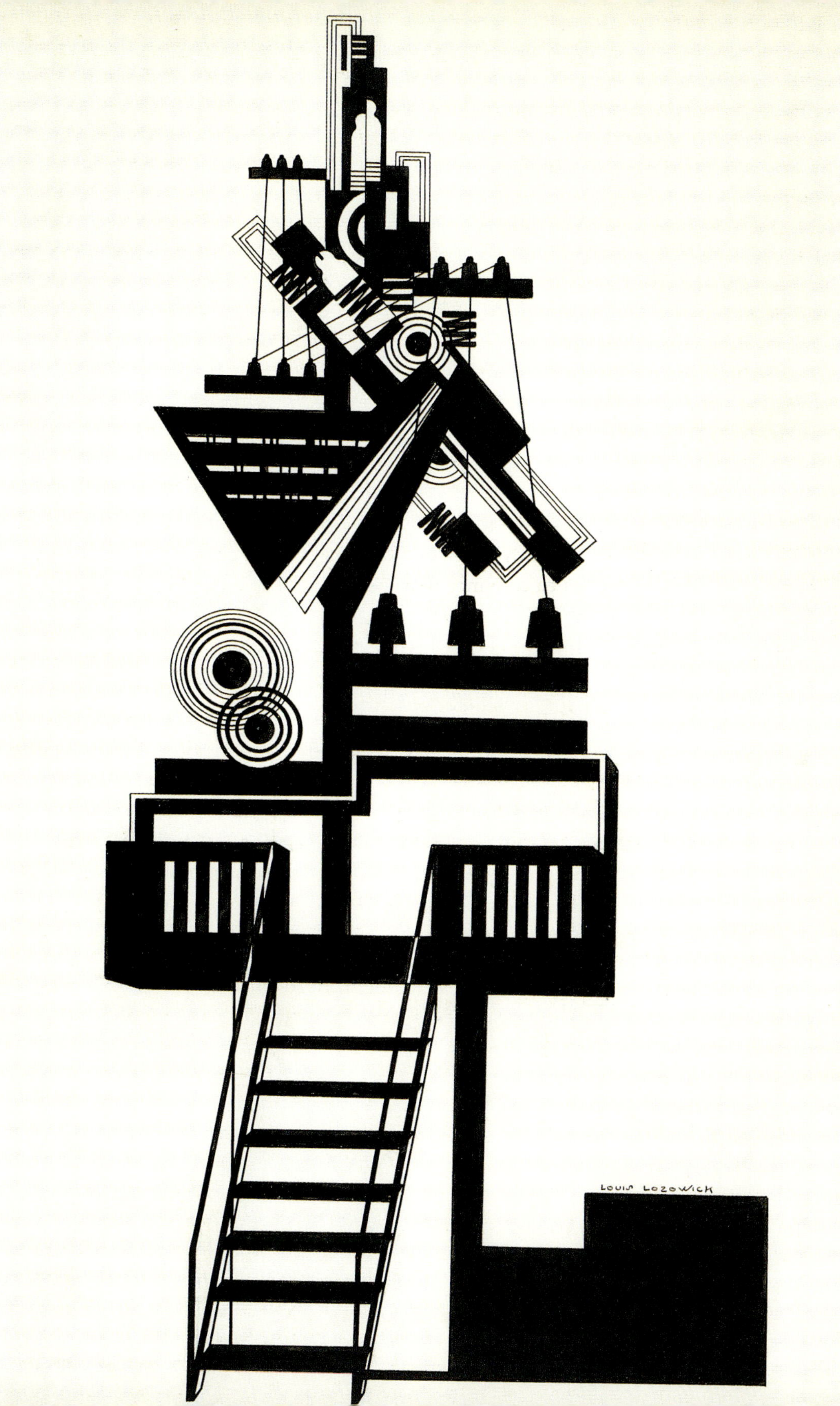
LOUIS LOZOWICK

**MAN RAY**

1890 USA–1976 France

## *Landscape (Paysage Fauve)*

1913
watercolor
13 7/8 x 9 3/4 in.
Smithsonian American Art Museum, Gift of the Man Ray Trust

One of the most highly abstracted compositions of his early career, *Landscape (Paysage Fauve)* marks an important stage in Man Ray's rapid development as a leading modernist artist. He was given his first one-man show of paintings in New York at the Charles Daniel's gallery shortly after the completion of this work. *Fauve,* French for "wild beast," was used as a pejorative title for a group of early-twentieth-century artists who used bright, non-descriptive colors in their art. The dark outlines and simplified forms of this composition reflect his decision to abandon the direct observation of nature in favor of a more spontaneous, imaginative rendition. He transforms the traditional landscape elements of land, horizon, and sky into a brilliant, jewel-like composition of curvilinear forms that bear little resemblance to an actual place but instead convey an exquisite landscape's startling beauty.

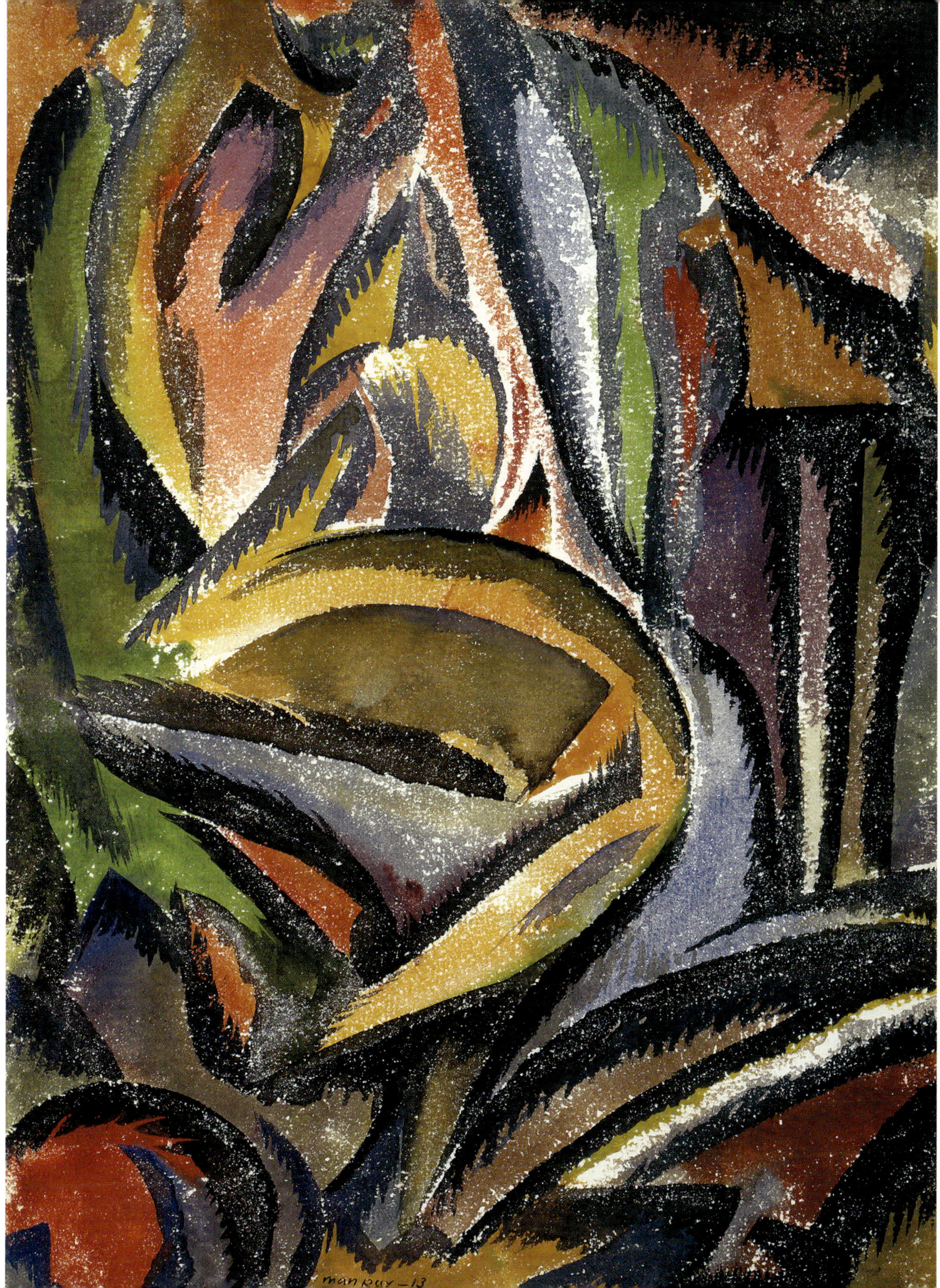
man ray – 13

**JOHN MARIN**

1870–1953

## *The Sea, Maine*

1921
watercolor and charcoal
16 ½ x 19 ⅝ in.
Smithsonian American Art Museum

*The Sea, Maine* is a quintessential expression of John Marin's most enduring interests. He spent part of almost every year in Maine from 1914 until his death, and painted seascapes of its rugged coast throughout his career. He was less interested in portraying specific, recognizable sites than in conveying the forces of nature along the rocky, untamed Maine coast. In this dynamic composition, the rhythmic crashing of waves in the middle ground contrasts with the calmer, deep blue of the horizon as well as with the solid, curvilinear rock forms in the foreground. Marin's calligraphic lines suggest movement and energy rather than superficial appearances. A master of the watercolor technique, he varied his application of color from thin, transparent washes to dense, opaque strokes and more solid areas of coverage. As one of America's leading abstract artists, Marin transformed a traditional subject into a modernist idiom.

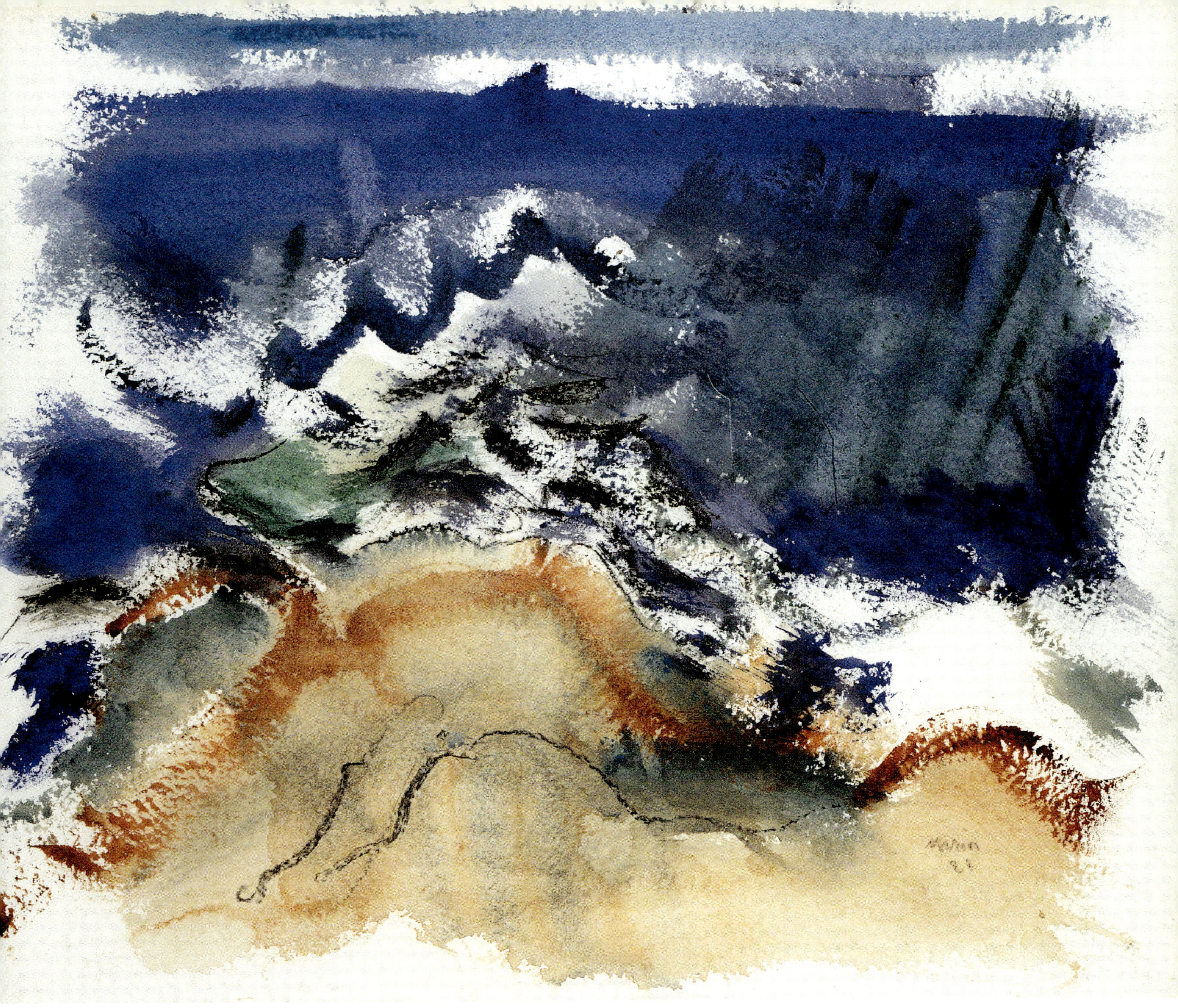

**THOMAS MORAN**

1837 England–1926 USA

## *Above Tower Falls, Yellowstone*

1872
watercolor and gouache
15 x 10 ½ in.
Smithsonian American Art Museum, Gift of Mrs. Armistead Peter III

Tower Falls is a spectacular, 156-foot waterfall in Montana's Yellowstone Park, where Thomas Moran accompanied a survey party led by Dr. Ferdinand V. Hayden for the United States Geological Survey in 1872. The waterfall's name refers not only to the stunning height of the formation, but also to the spire-like rock pinnacles at its top. Moran suggests the staggering height of the falls in his composition by the sense of a deep precipice beyond the urgent water.

The survey was an exciting adventure and an important scientific project. The falls had been documented by visitors from the earliest trips of Europeans into the region. The survey group traveled through the park on horseback, and Moran often had only a brief period of time to capture his impressions of a site in a quick, black-and-white sketch. When they returned to camp, he would add a small amount of color to his sketches. This highly finished and detailed watercolor of Tower Falls was probably created back in his studio, based on numerous field sketches. Moran's paintings and watercolors were instrumental in the establishment of Yellowstone National Park.

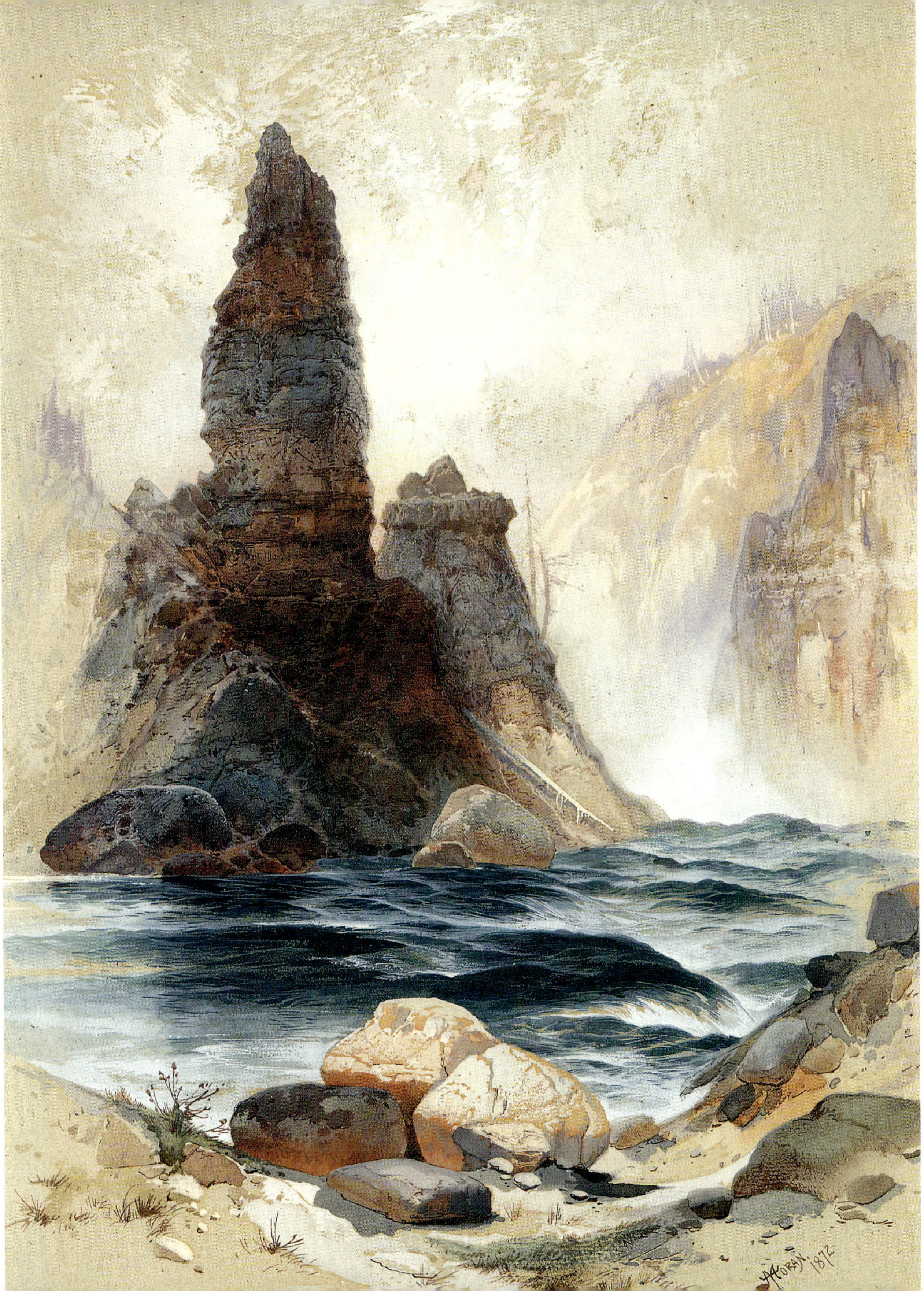
TMORAN. 1872

**THOMAS MORAN**

1837 England–1926 USA

## *Shin-Au-Av-Tu-Weap (God Land), Cañon of the Colorado. Utah Territory*

about 1872–73
watercolor and pencil
4 ¾ x 14 ½ in.
Smithsonian American Art Museum, Gift of Dr. William Henry Holmes

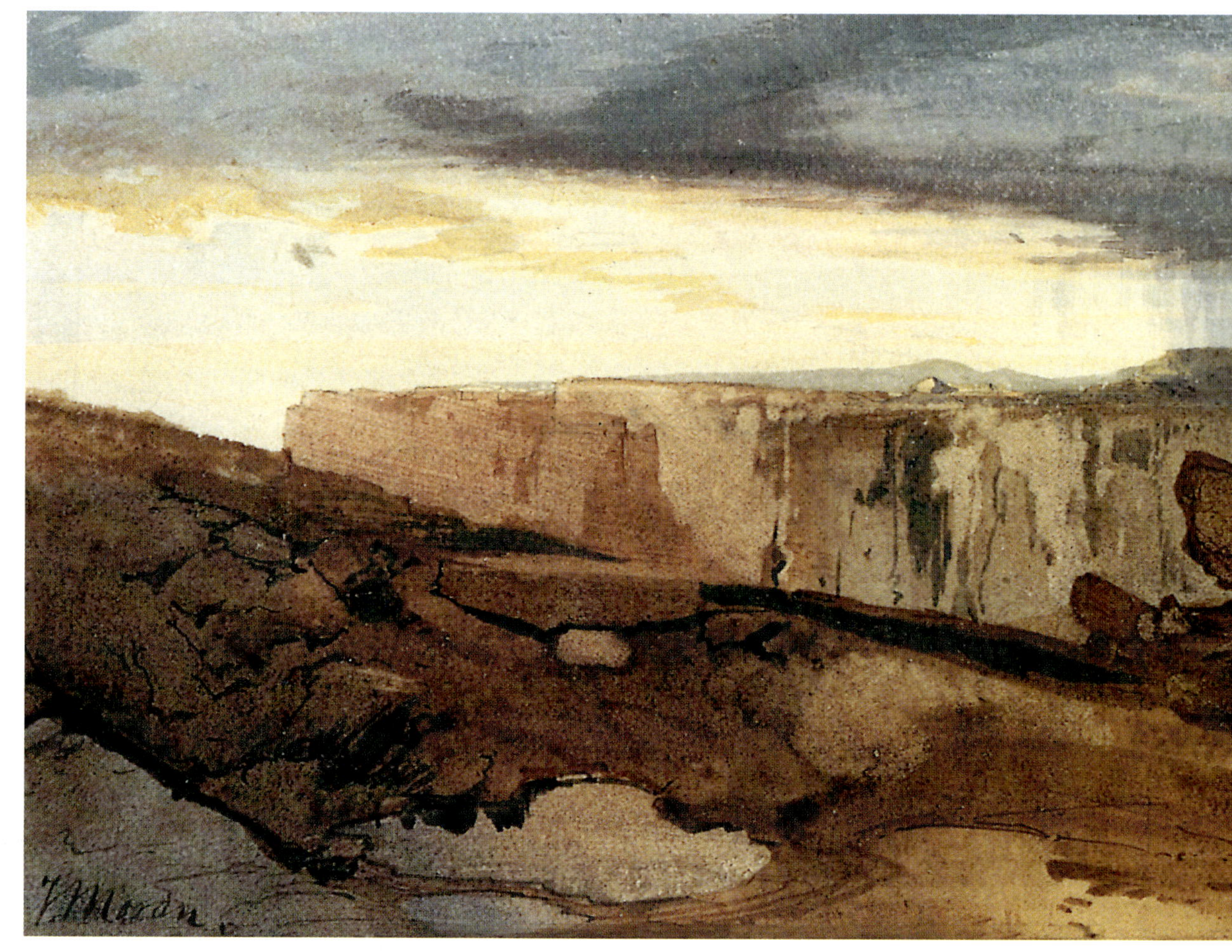

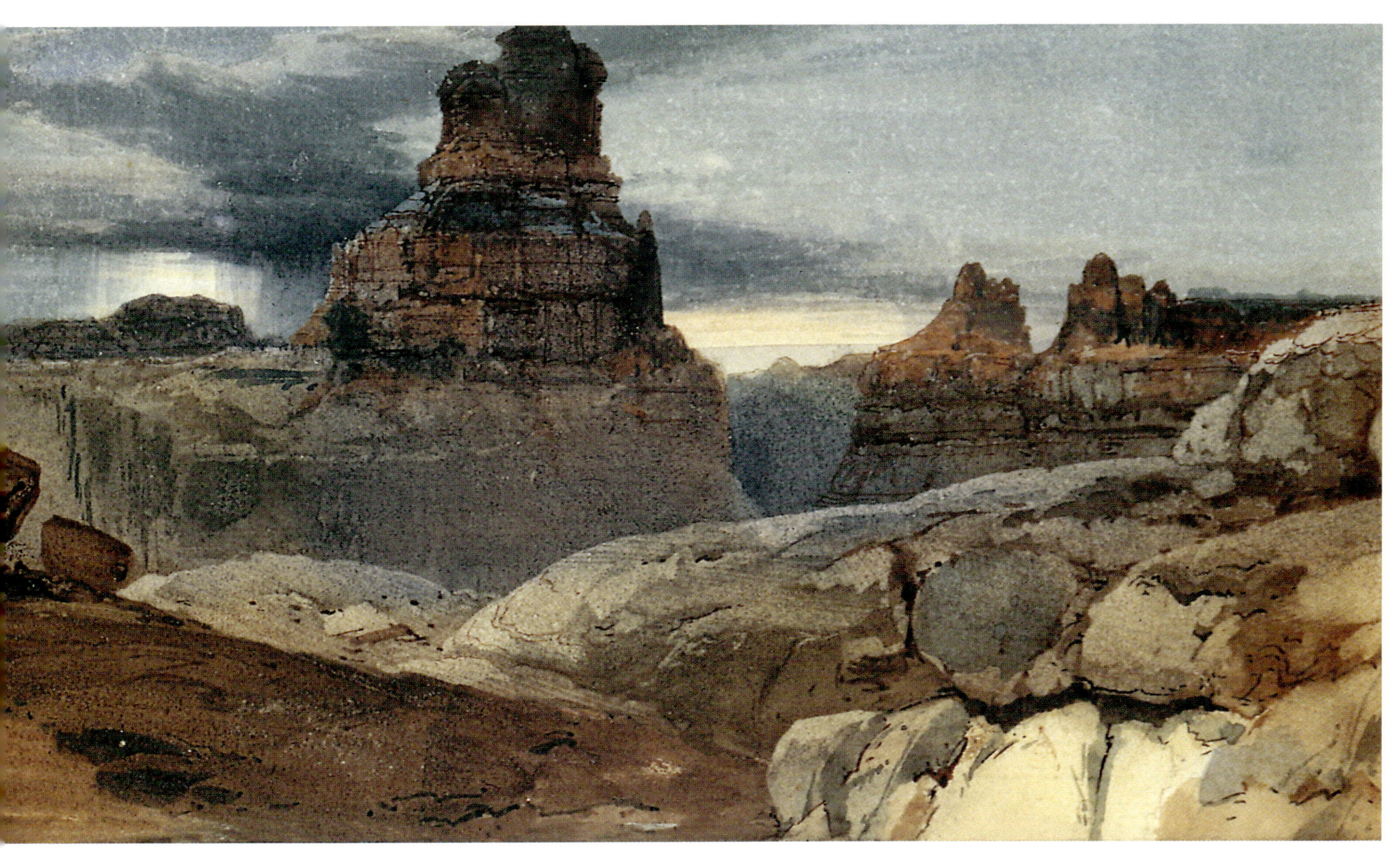

**GLADYS NILSSON**

born 1940

## *Arytystic Pairanoiya*

1978
watercolor and pencil
25 1/4 x 40 3/8 in.
Smithsonian American Art Museum, Gift of the S. W. and B. M. Koffler Foundation

A humorous vignette with bright, primary colors and cartoon-like figures, Gladys Nilsson's watercolor *Arytystic Pairanoiya* defies easy interpretation, as its inventive title would lead one to believe. The title does provides some clues, but the meaning remains open to the viewer's imagination. "Arytystic" sounds like artist or artistic, suggesting that one of the two large, female figures represents the artist herself, embraced by a single male figure. Are the two large female figures the artist and her alter-ego? "Pairanoiya" calls our attention to the pairs of figures throughout the composition, at the same time that it refers to the mental state of paranoia. The oval shape in the yellow figure's hand resembles a pocket mirror, in which the artist sees a pathetic, kneeling figure. The exaggerated forms, impossible space, and multiplicity of details suggest the tragicomic chaos of the human condition.

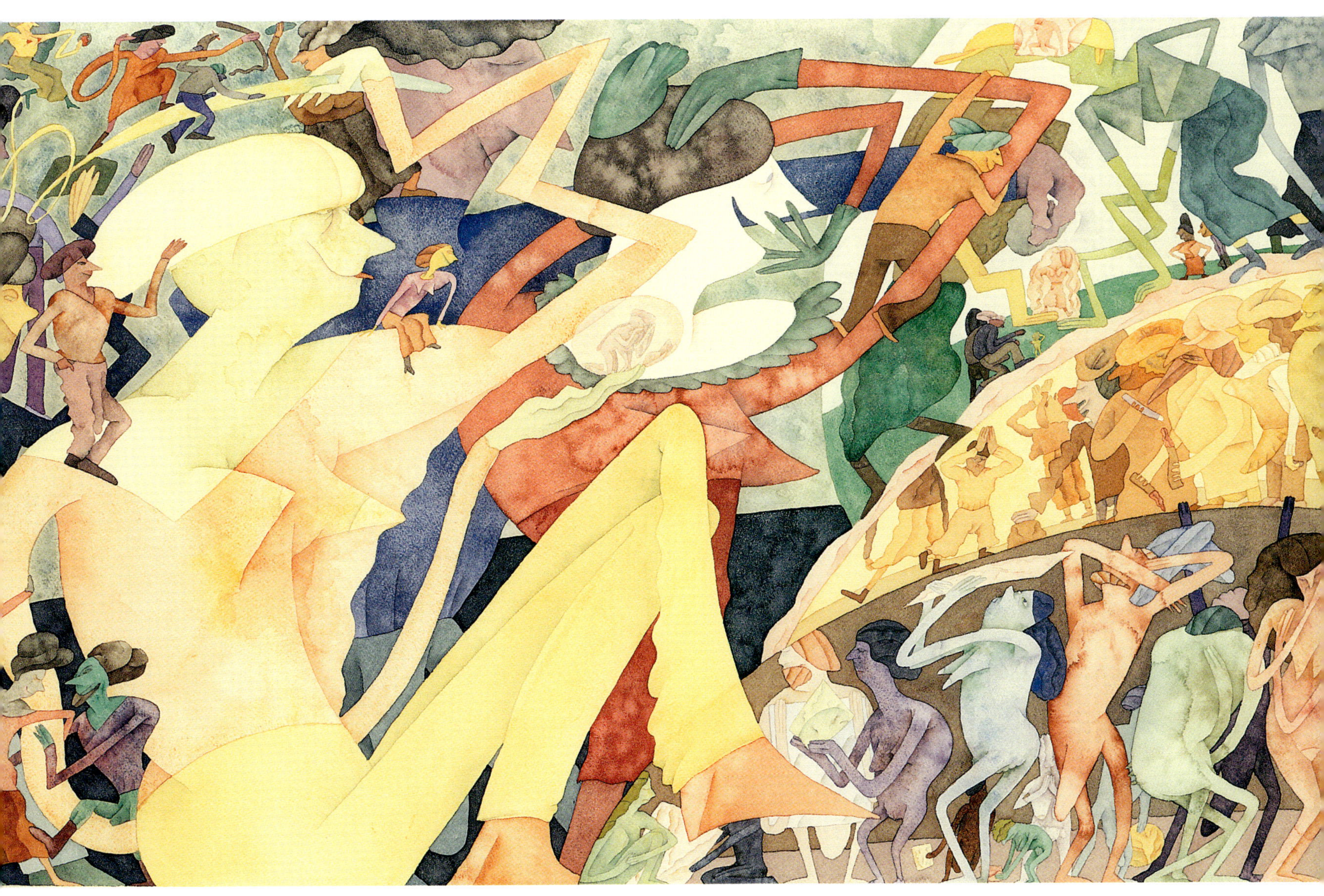

## MAXFIELD PARRISH

1870–1966

# *"What they talked about"—"They make me walk behind, 'cos they say I'm too little, and musn't hear..."*

1899
pencil, chalk, pen and ink, and ink wash
11 5/8 x 7 1/2 in.
Smithsonian American Art Museum, Bequest of Olin Dows

This charming young girl, Charlotte, is one of thirty-two illustrations drawn by Maxfield Parrish for English writer Kenneth Grahame's *The Golden Age*, which was published simultaneously in New York and London. Written for older children and adults, the book is about four children in an English country family whose fantasies about the adult world are the subjects for the individual chapters and episodes. Parrish depicts the experiences of childhood from the perspective of an adult nostalgic for an ideal world that never was. Although the girl is sad and momentarily isolated, she stands in an idyllic garden, protected by the two sturdy posts that flank her. She seems poised in the portal between childhood and adolescence. Parrish used the text as a point of departure for his drawings, but he did not feel obliged to illustrate the scenes exactly as the author had described them.

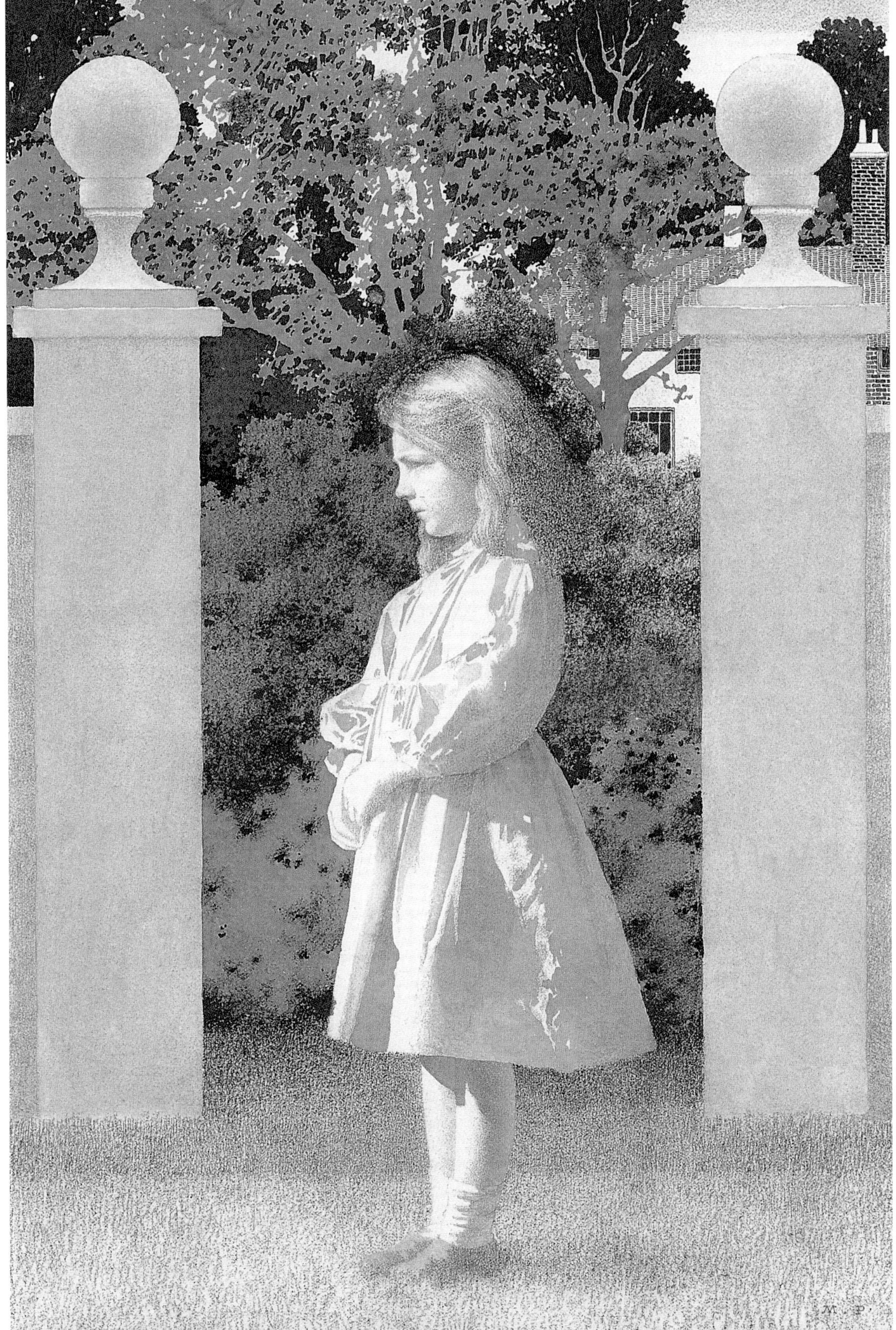
M · P

**CHARLES SELIGER**

born 1926

## *Celestial*

1956
pencil, tempera, oil, and wax
15 x 21 7/8 in.
Smithsonian American Art Museum, Gift of Mr. and Mrs. Hy Klebanow

Charles Seliger's abstract, organic imagery reflects the natural world—earth strata, botanical and biological forms, primeval and oceanic life—yet the artist also has described his representations as "inner landscapes." *Celestial* refers to the heavens, which were among his many visual sources. The silvery delicacy of line and forms in this drawing suggest the invisible world made visible, blurring distinctions between microscopic images and views through a telescope. "The intricacies of structure within natural forms, animate my paintings and drawings. Beyond nature's recognizable appearances, the invisible reveals itself with its splendid complexities and remarkable truthfulness."

With no formal art training, Seliger instead studied art in the many museums and galleries of New York City. Looking at art from Coptic Egypt and Persian manuscript illumination to contemporary surrealism, he invented a language of abstract expression that emphasized the spiritual quality of natural phenomena.

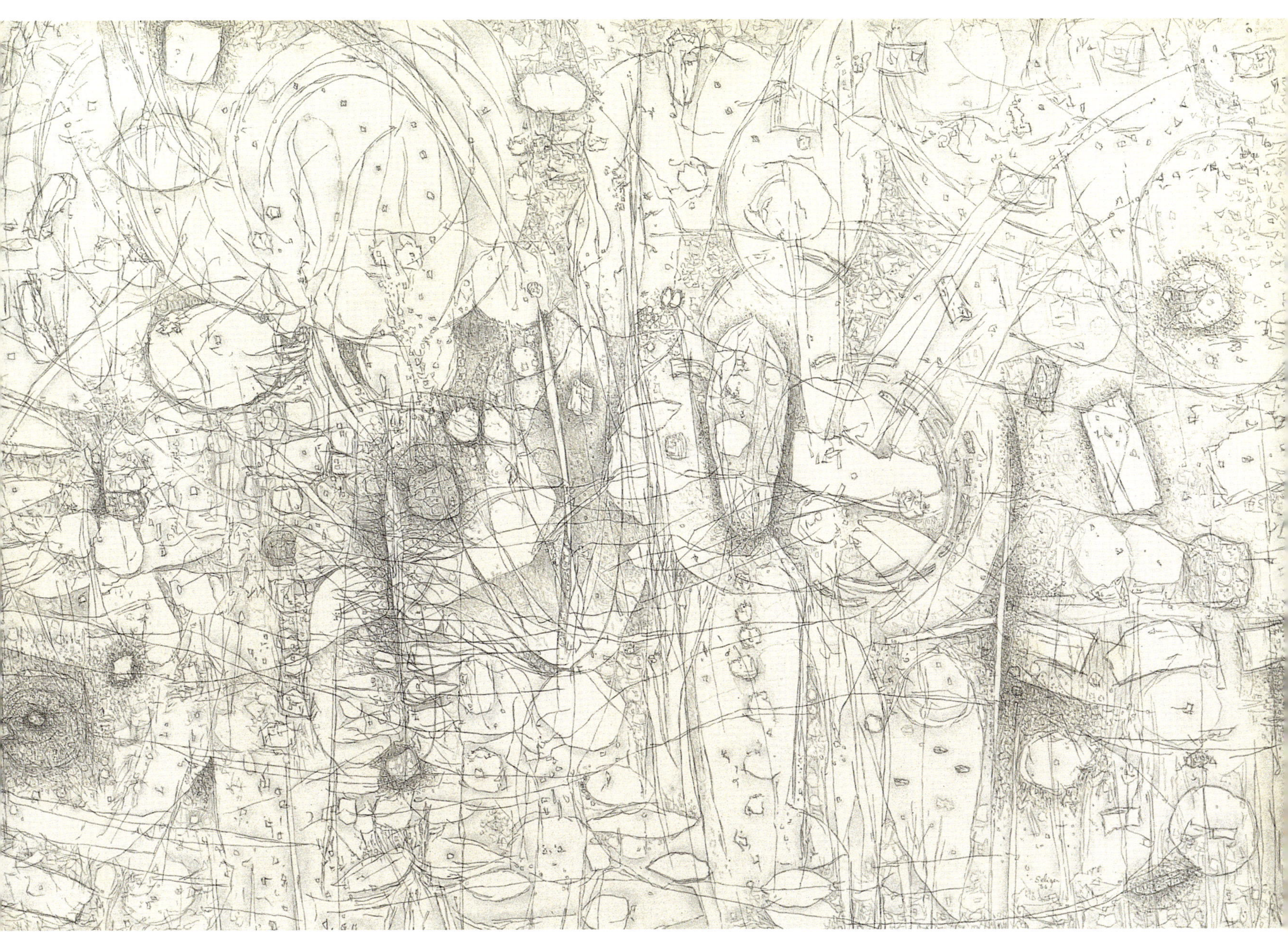

**EVERETT SHINN**

1876–1953

## *Eviction (Lower East Side)*

1904
gouache
8 3/8 x 13 1/8 in.
Smithsonian American Art Museum, Bequest of Henry Ward Ranger through the National Academy of Design

Everett Shinn's depiction of human shame and suffering in *Eviction* reveals his sympathy for the dispossessed. Witnessing the eviction of an old, bearded musician from his apartment on the Lower East Side may have inspired this dramatic depiction of misery. Shinn shows the dislocated family grouped on a mattress in postures of helplessness as bystanders watch the family's household possessions being removed from their home. He contrasts the suffering family with the bustling activity surrounding them. The policeman shown supervising the eviction clearly represents the offical stoicism. Drawing with short, lively strokes of paint, Shinn enlivens the surface and draws the viewer throughout the scene with touches of color and bright white highlights. His portrayals of the poor owe much to the manner in which popular photojournalistic investigations represented the realities of urban life.

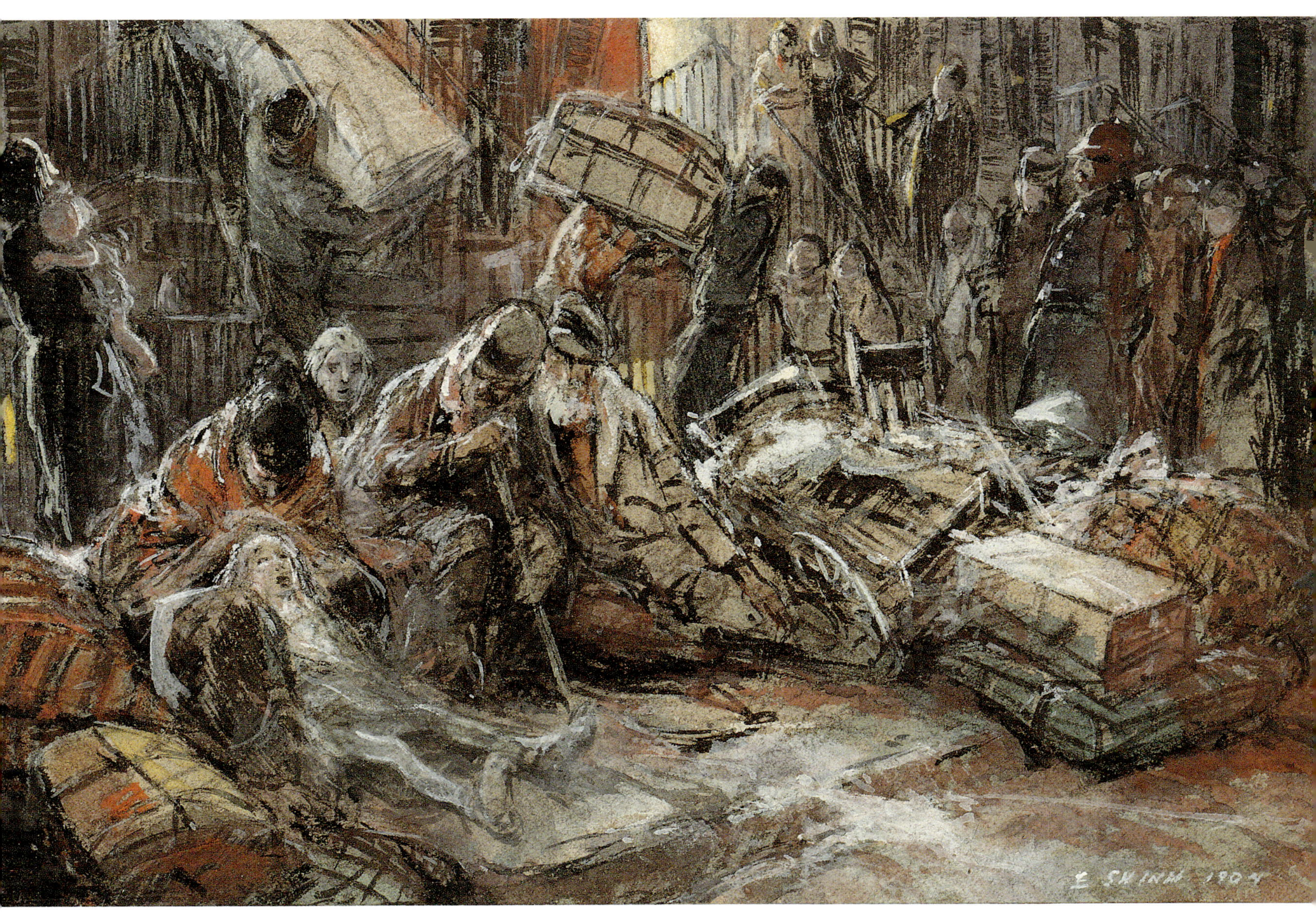
E. SHINN 1904

**DAVID SMITH**

1906–1965

## *Untitled*

about 1951
ink and tempera
18 ¼ x 23 ¼ in.
Smithsonian American Art Museum

With only the slightest suggestion of landscape in the curved and horizontal lines of the lower part of this composition, the artist draws bold, abstract lines that suggest organic forms and lively motion, like birds in flight and trees swaying in the wind. The touches of blue tempera enliven the lines at the same time they declare this drawing to be one of his intentionally finished pieces. Smith explained his fascination with the immediacy of drawing: "More his truth than other media, . . . more his truth than words can express, drawing more shaped like he is shaped, because the pressure of performance hasn't made him something he isn't."

David Smith, son and grandson of blacksmiths, is known primarily as a sculptor. However, he made drawings throughout his career, often as studies for his sculpture, but occasionally as independent works of art.

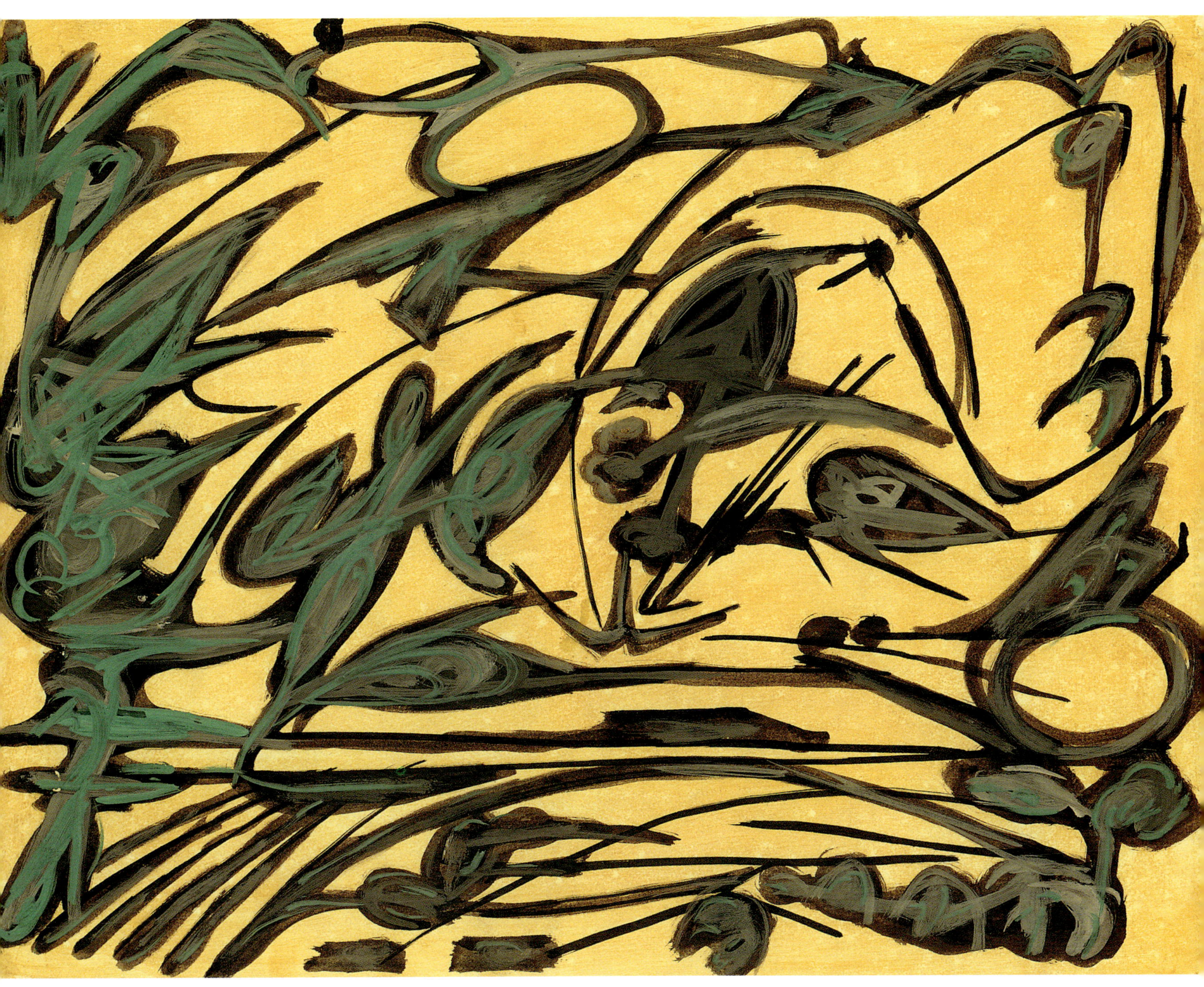

**SAUL STEINBERG**

1914 Romania–1999 USA

## *Still Life with Cat*

1966
pen and ink, ink wash, colored pencil, pencil, and collage
23 3/8 x 29 3/8 in.
Smithsonian American Art Museum, Gift of the artist

Saul Steinberg has described himself as "a writer who can't write. The line . . . is my real language." As a cartoonist whose drawings regularly appeared in the *New Yorker,* Steinberg elevated comic illustration to a fine art. *Still Life with Cat* refers to the centuries-long tradition of still life painting, but Steinberg turns this tradition on its head by relying strictly on his imagination rather than observation. The two blue-and-white porcelain vases, as well as the book and the table, recall traditional still life elements, but all the other forms are imaginative creations that merely suggest real objects. The cat's face has a dead-pan human profile, and perhaps refers to the artist himself. When one looks to the writing in the drawing for an explanation of the enigmatic imagery, it is legible only as lines drawn to mimic writing.

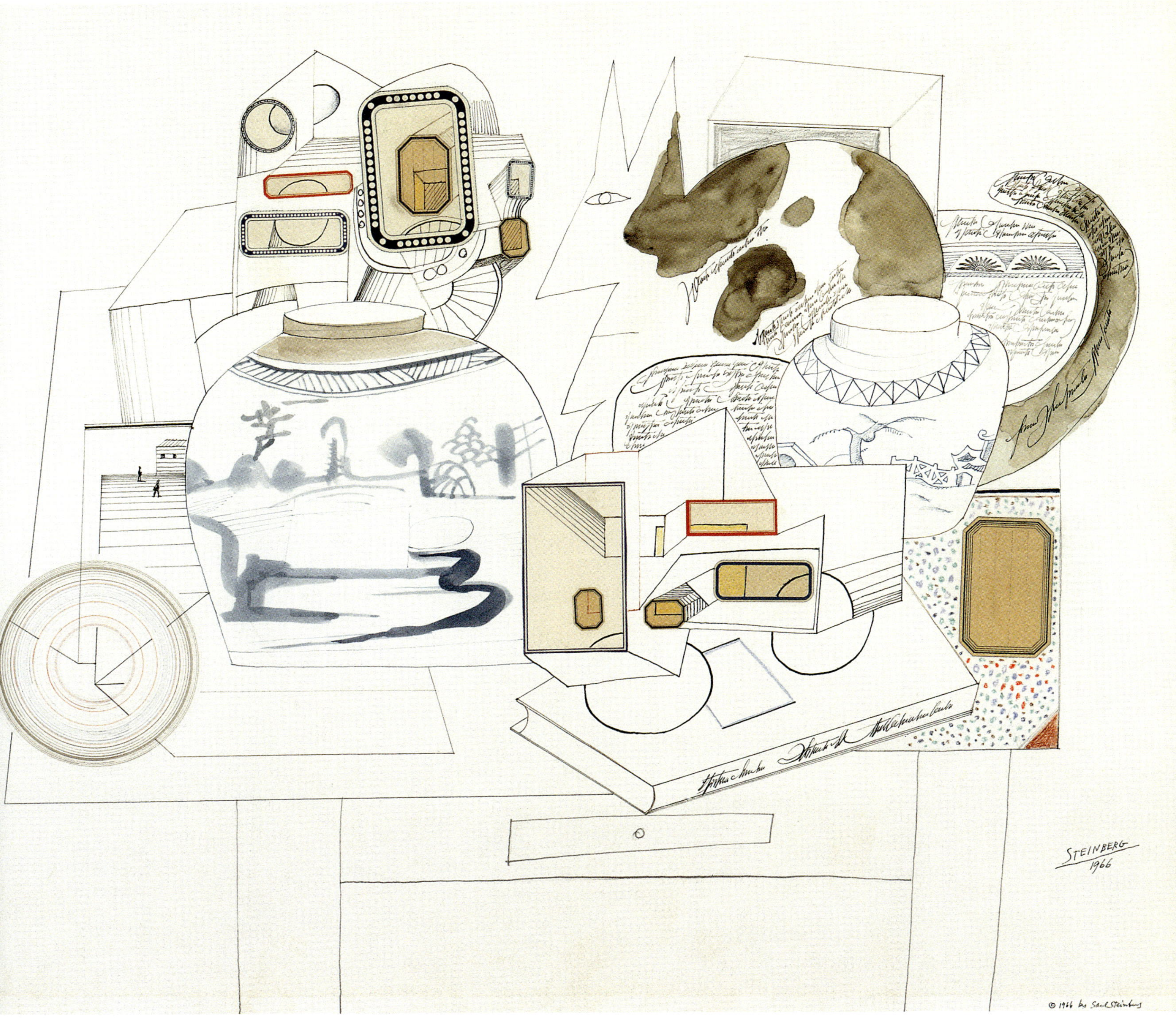
STEINBERG
1966

**JOSEPH STELLA**

1877 Italy–1946 USA

## *Flower Study*

about 1919
silverpoint and crayon
12 7/8 x 6 1/2 in.
Smithsonian American Art Museum, purchase through the Robert Tyler Davis Memorial Fund

Throughout a career as one of America's leading early abstract artists, Joseph Stella retained a strong interest in depicting nature. Exquisite drawings of flowers, birds, and trees made up an important segment of his work on paper, and frequently served as studies for segments of his large, complex paintings. The care and attention he lavished on these drawings, however, suggest that he valued them as finished works of art.

In contrast to pencil drawings, silverpoint lines are made by dragging a stylus with a silver tip across the surface of specially prepared paper. The pressure of the silverpoint stylus creates a slight incision in the prepared ground that cannot be erased or covered up, requiring certainty and precision on the part of the artist. Stella chose silverpoint for many of his nature studies because he relished the challenge this technique presented as well as the exquisite delicacy of its line. "I was seized with a sensual thrill in cutting with the sharpness of my silverpoint the terse purity of the lotus leaves or the matchless stem of a strange tropical plant."

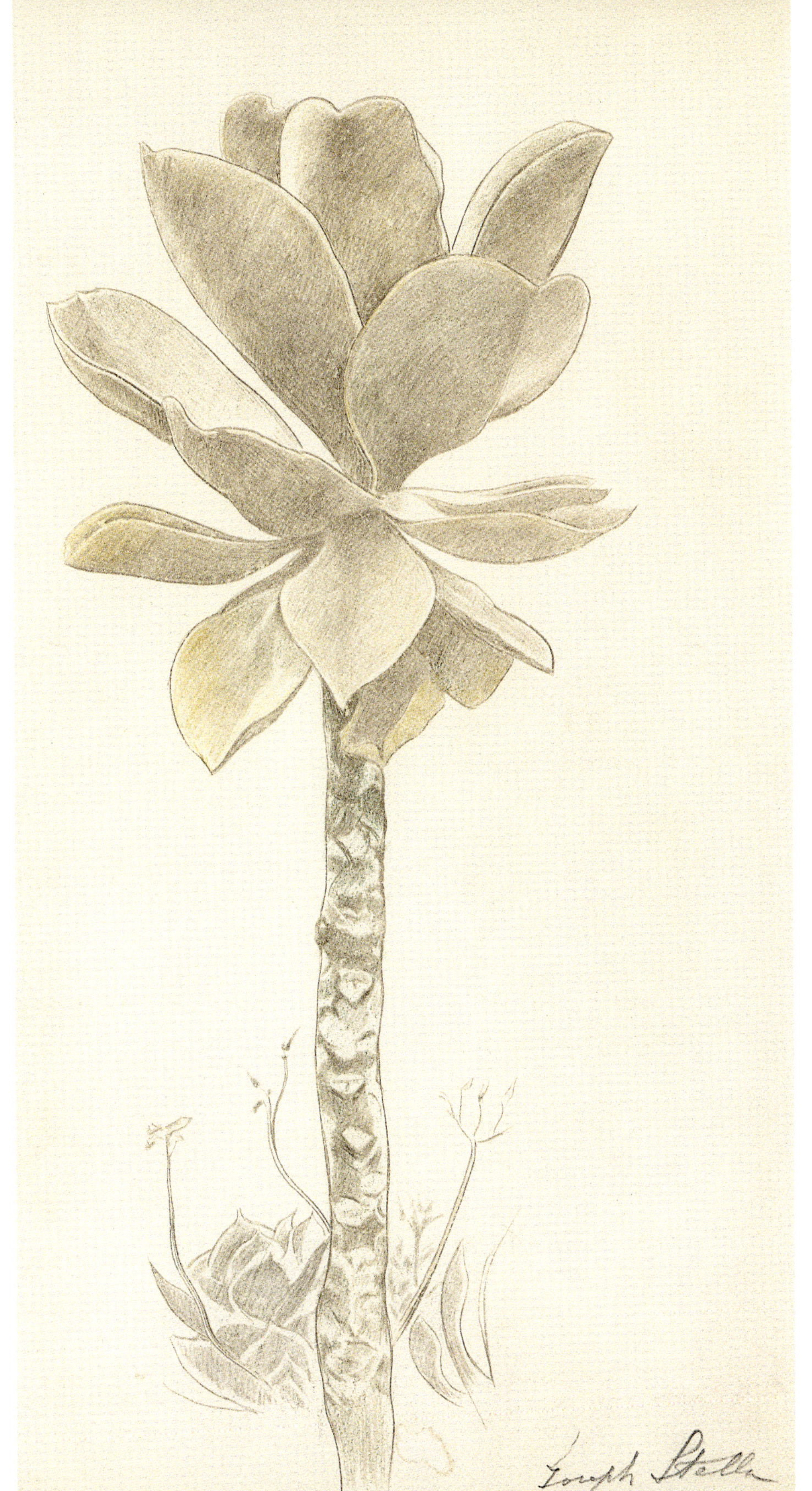
Joseph Stella

**HENRY OSSAWA TANNER**

1859 USA–1937 France

# *Study for Rachel*

## from *The Mothers of the Bible*

about 1898
charcoal
23 x 13 5/8 in.
Smithsonian American Art Museum, Gift of Mr. and Mrs. Norman Robbins

Henry Ossawa Tanner had been married less than three years at the time he drew this image, and the model might well have been the artist's wife, Jessie Olssen. *Study for Rachel* is a sketch for one of four works featuring Sarah, Hagar, Rachel, and Mary, called "The Mothers of the Bible," which Tanner published in the *Ladies Home Journal.* He wrote captions for each painting in the series. Rachel was the bride-to-be of Jacob, and turning to Genesis (29:10–11), Tanner sought "to present the story in the picture [as] a love story of Biblical times with the fresh human interest of all times preserved." The artist, whose father was the Reverend Benjamin Tanner, was raised in a very religious African American family, which strongly influenced his interest in biblical subject matter.

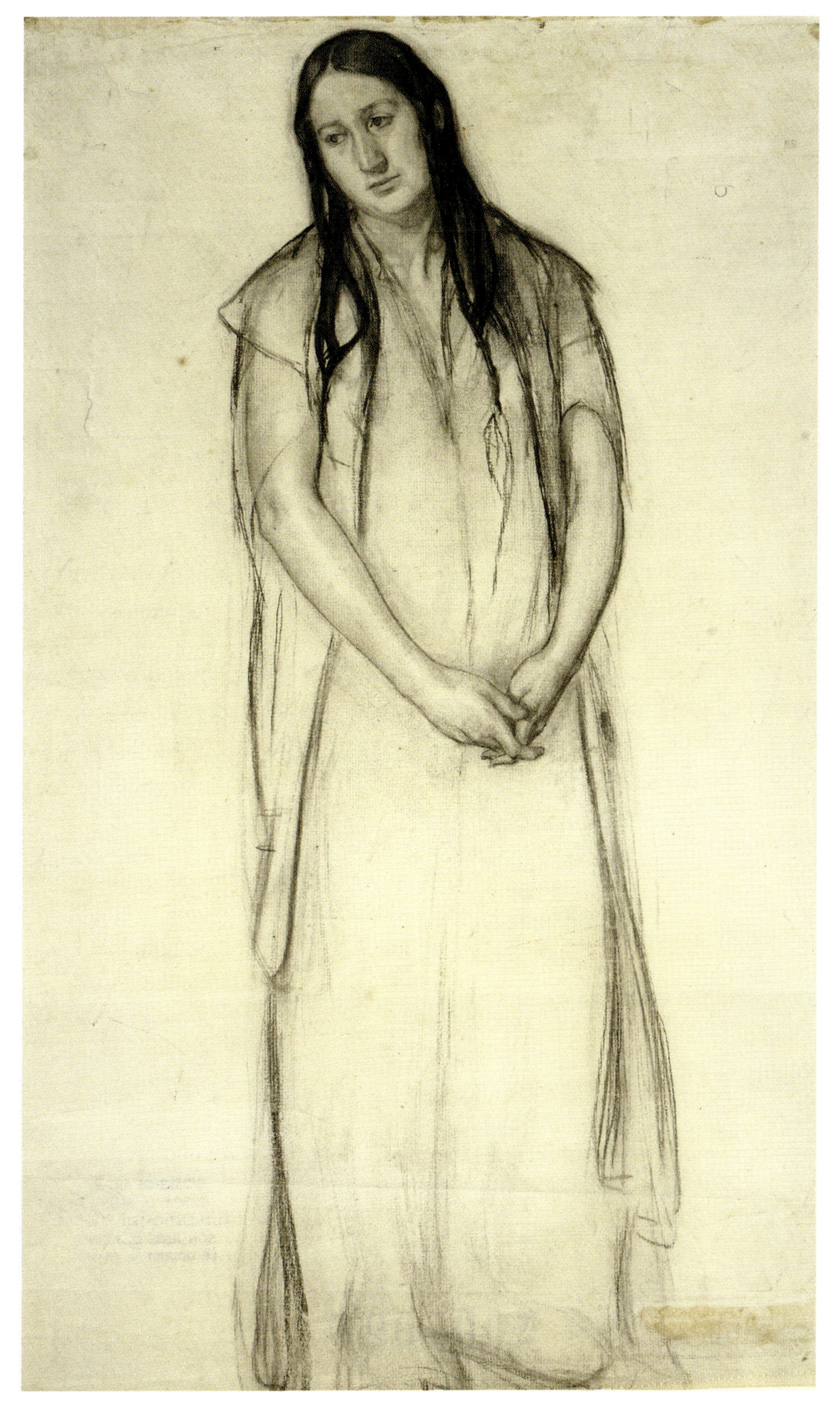

**MASAMI TERAOKA**

born Japan 1936

## *Oiran and Mirror*

### from the *AIDS Series*

1988
watercolor
15 x 22 ¼ in.
Smithsonian American Art Museum, purchase made possible by Eugene Vail, Martha Loomis, Mrs. Rhinelander Stewart and Mrs. E. N. Vanderpoel

"The basis of my work, the humor and seriousness of two cultures—East and West—clashing, is provided by my own life experiences. . . . In my work I take the best and worst of both cultures and juxtapose them in a coherent statement that is visually exhilarating." In 1986 Teraoka met an old friend who had become infected with AIDS as a result of a blood transfusion and who had a newborn baby. By focusing on this disease in an extended series of paintings, watercolors, and prints, Teraoka sought to draw attention to the social and health issues raised by this modern plague.

The Japanese writing in the background of *Oiran and Mirror* translates: "Pretty soon my boyfriend will be here. I wonder if he is prepared with a condom. Even if I have visited Anzenji Shrine [Geishas often go to shrines to pray for safety], maybe I should use a woman's condom. Oh, the telephone is ringing." Her boyfriend, shown in the mirror, is calling. He tells her, "I have to work late again tonight." By imitating the traditional style of Ukiyo-e, "the floating world" of nineteenth-century Japanese painting and woodblock prints, he transforms the anxiety of contemporary life into a kind of visual Kabuki theater, full of drama, elegance, and pop irony.

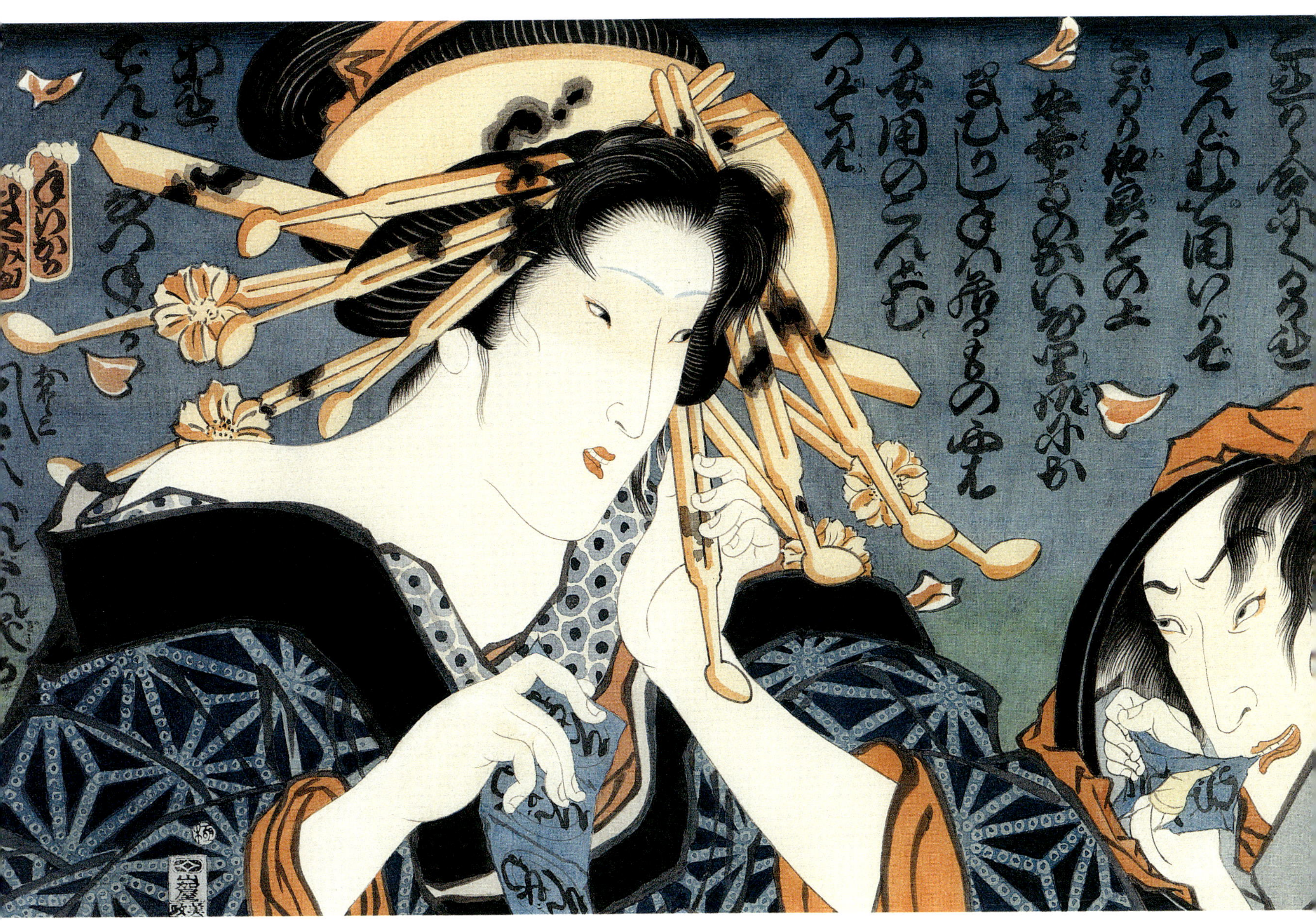

**WAYNE THIEBAUD**

born 1920

## *Neapolitan Meringue*

1986–99
pastel over lithograph
14 x 16 ½ in.
Smithsonian American Art Museum, Gift of Warren Unna, Terry and Margaret Stent, and the Thiebaud Family, and museum purchase in honor of Nan Tucker McEvoy

Wayne Thiebaud endows his subjects with a sense of joy and eloquence. The artist is usually attracted to specific foods by their formal beauty, and by the care with which the chef has prepared and presented the item. In *Neapolitan Meringue,* Thiebaud relishes how the meringue topping simultaneously glows and reflects light, suggesting the softness of a snowbank and the rich sensuality of white paint. An uncut pastry's perfection would make it seem inaccessible—the missing slice here reveals the luscious layers within, and tempts us to trim a little of the topping for a surreptitious taste.

An artist who moves easily from painting to drawing to printmaking, Thiebaud has made use of his black-and-white prints to rethink images through the addition of color. He created *Neapolitan Meringue* in 1999 as a pastel drawing over a lithograph from 1986, enhancing the spare, linear composition with the immediacy of the artist's touch and sensual texture. Thiebaud obliterates the lithographic lines under a dense layer of powdery pastel to transform a familiar composition into a rich variation on a theme.

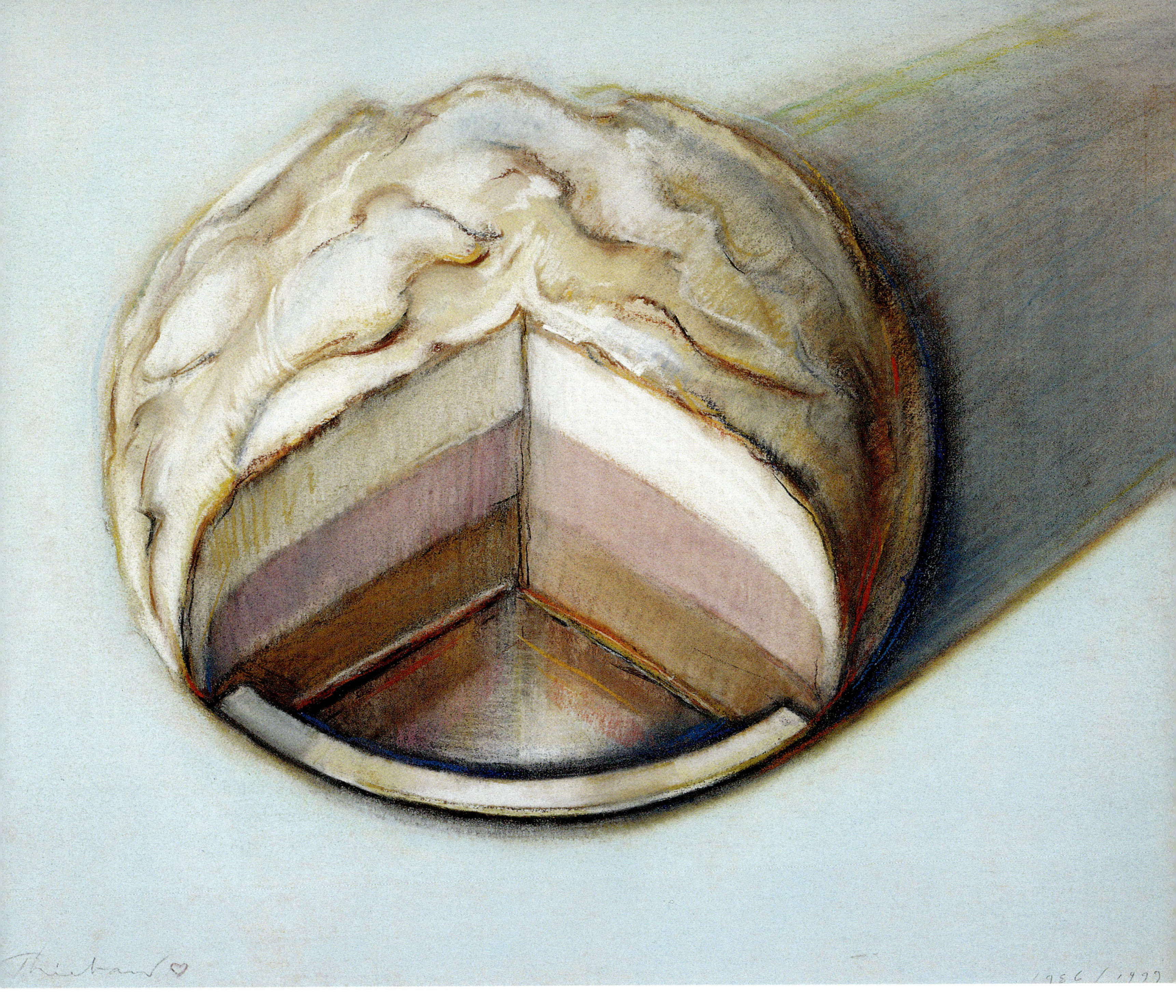

**MARK TOBEY**

1890 USA–1976 Switzerland

# *Canticle*

1954
casein
17 3/4 x 11 5/8 in.
Smithsonian American Art Museum, Gift of the Sara Roby Foundation

Abstraction and spirituality are intimately entwined in the mature work of Mark Tobey. The title *Canticle* refers to liturgical hymns taken from the Bible and used in church services. Tobey pointed to the abstractness and harmony of music as an important source of inspiration: "When I play the piano for several hours, everything is clarified in my visual imagination afterwards."

Tobey's expression of spirituality was framed to be more universal than that associated with any specific religion. He followed the Baha'i faith, which teaches the unity of the world and the oneness of mankind, and borrows elements from many different religions. As Tobey stated, "I've tried to decentralize and interpenetrate so that all parts of a painting are of equal value." The intricate pattern of light-colored calligraphic symbols that animates the abstract surface of this work came to be known as "white writing," and was inspired by the artist's study of Arabic and Japanese calligraphy.

**JOHN HENRY TWACHTMAN**
1853–1902

# *Haystacks at Edge of Woods*

about 1895
pastel
9 5/8 x 14 1/8 in.
Smithsonian American Art Museum, Gift of John Gellatly

John Twachtman delighted in depicting his home in Greenwich, Connecticut, especially its gardens and surrounding seventeen acres of land. He was particularly fond of scenes, such as *Haystacks at Edge of Woods,* that showed nature in its wild state punctuated with accents of human habitation and cultivation. His practice of working out of doors emphasized the effects of sunlight and atmosphere on the scenes he was depicting. During his Greenwich period, experiments with impressionist techniques were combined with structured compositions and a strong sense of design.

For a significant portion of his career, Twachtman worked simultaneously in pastel and oil, with pastel drawings often garnering more critical attention than his paintings. Critics were especially intrigued by his distinctive method of drawing on papers of different hues and leaving large areas of the paper relatively bare, with only delicate suggestions of color and form.

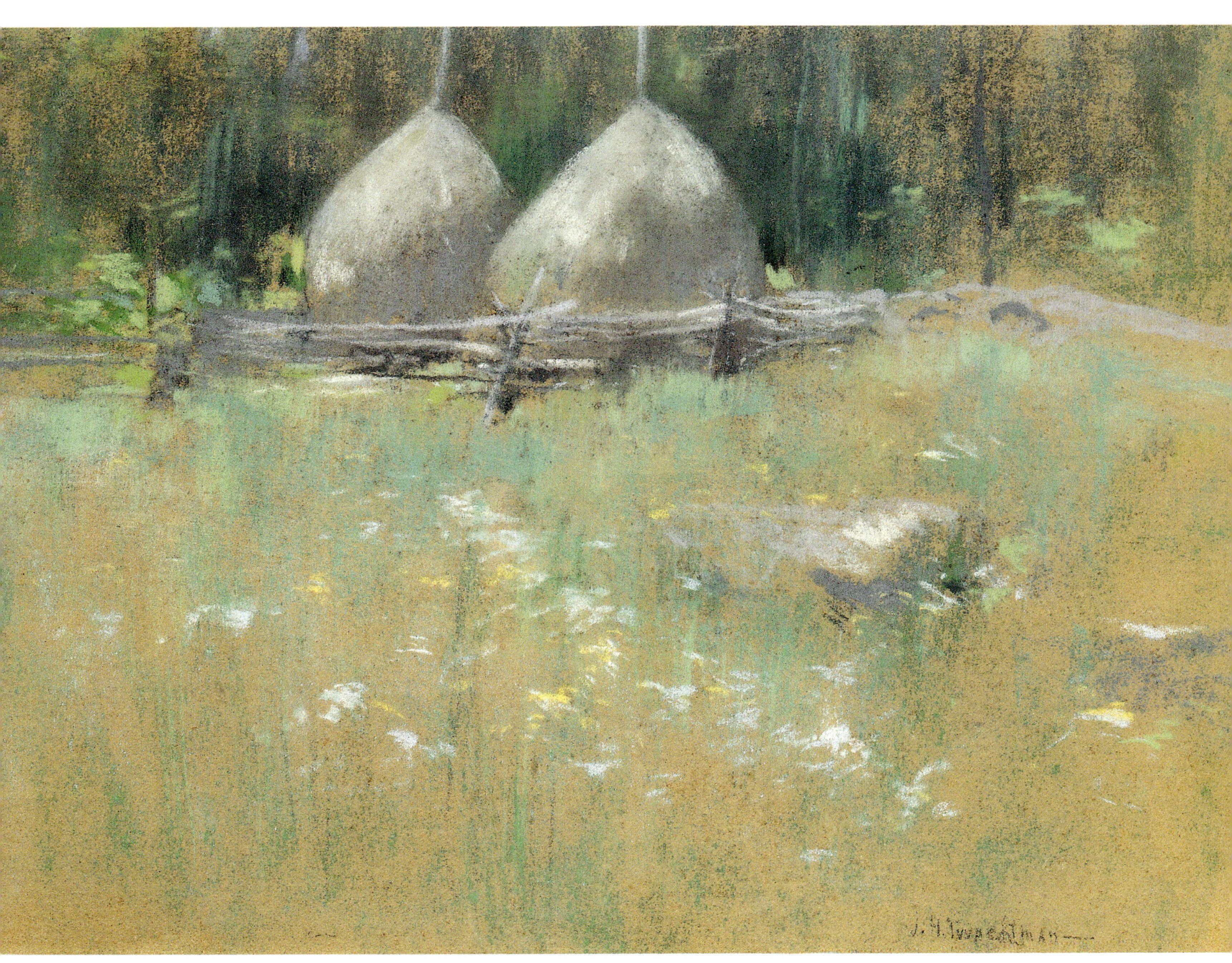

**ELIHU VEDDER**

1836 USA–1923 Italy

# *The Cup of Death*

## Illustration for *Rubáiyát of Omar Khayyám*

1883–84
chalk, pencil, and ink
19 3⁄8 x 14 7⁄8 in.
Smithsonian American Art Museum, purchase and gift from Elizabeth W. Henderson in memory of her husband Francis Tracy Henderson

The verses illustrated by Elihu Vedder were written by the twelfth-century Persian mathematician, astronomer, and poet Omar Khayyám. A large selection of his poems was translated into English in the mid-nineteenth century, and acquired an ardent following among artists, such as Vedder, who sought spiritual and poetic values in a time of rampant materialism. The themes of fate, death, and the renewal of life were especially poignant for Vedder, who had recently experienced the death of two of his children and the birth of two more.

When the first edition of his illustrated *Rubáiyát of Omar Khayyám* was published in 1884, it sold out in six days! Critics acclaimed it a masterpiece of American art, and Vedder the leading American artist. It was so widely admired that it set the standard for the artist-designed book in America and England.

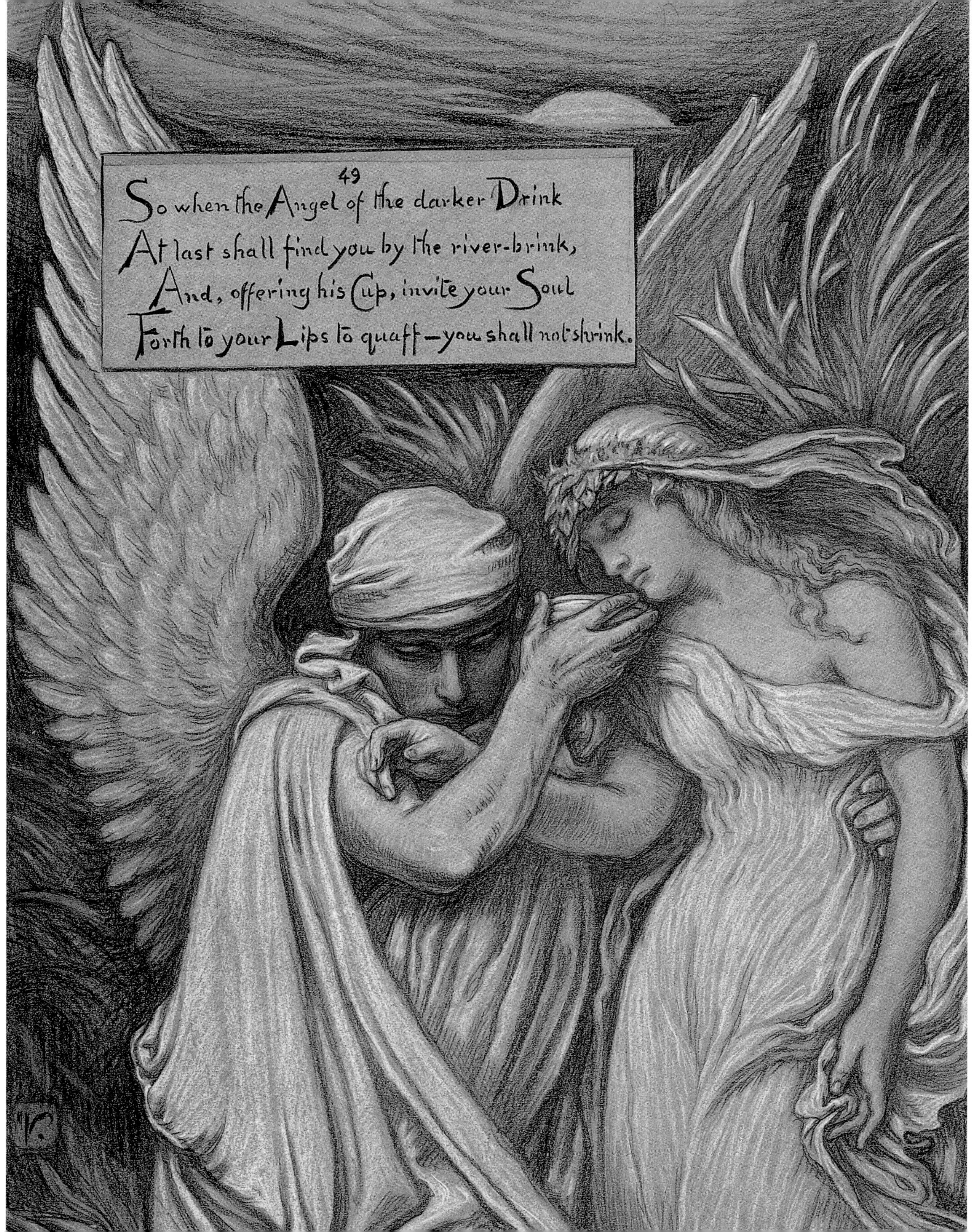
49
So when the Angel of the darker Drink
At last shall find you by the river-brink,
And, offering his Cup, invite your Soul
Forth to your Lips to quaff—you shall not shrink.

**MAX WEBER**

1881 Russia–1961 USA

## *Foundry in Baltimore*

1915
pastel
24 3/8 x 18 3/4 in.
Smithsonian American Art Museum

Max Weber visited Baltimore in 1915 when a gallery exhibited a group of his works. In an interview during that visit he declared: "My sole desire is to express myself; to paint what I see not with my eye, but with my consciousness." Perhaps that explains why the architectural motif in the upper portion of this composition so little resembles a foundry. Instead, the glowing colors, repeated curvilinear forms, and strongly vertical movement evoke a sense of spirituality rarely associated with industrial architecture. Nestled in a setting of trees and greenery, the composition suggests a utopian vision of industry in harmony with nature.

Weber had returned to New York in 1909 after a three-year stay in Paris. He was impressed with the vitality of urban America. With Europe in the throes of World War I, America represented progress and the future, which Weber expressed through the interpenetrating planes, abstracted forms, ambiguous space, and imaginative colors that convey his feelings about a scene, rather than its appearance.

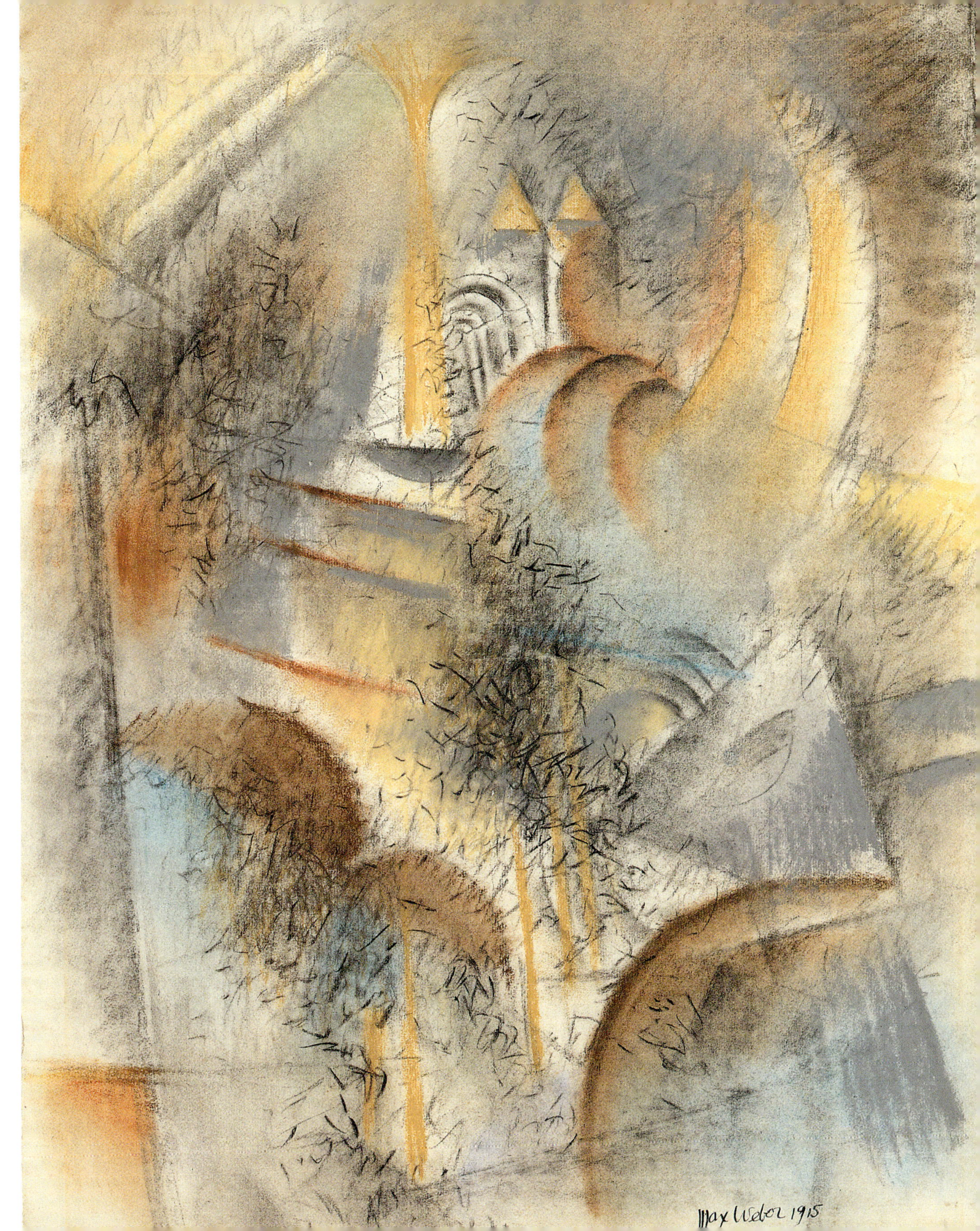
Max Weber 1915

**WILLIAM T. WILEY**

born 1937

## *Portrait of Radon*

1982
watercolor,
felt-tipped pen,
and ink
22 1/4 x 29 7/8 in.
Smithsonian
American Art
Museum

William Wiley's humorous and quirky parody of a map of the United States carries dark meanings beneath its cartoon-like surface. Wiley grew up in Richland, Washington, site of the U.S. government's Hanford Atomic Works, a plutonium production plant. This plant's legacy was a massive amount of radioactive waste that contaminated the surrounding area. The dark, diagonal line stretching from New York to Los Angeles represents a virtual highway—twelve lanes wide and one foot deep—constructed of radioactive tailings from the country's nuclear power plants.

Radon, a colorless, odorless, radioactive gas exuded by these tailings, also appeared in the news in the early 1980s as a naturally occurring gas that could seep into houses through cracks in their foundations. Wiley's verbal pun on the title in the lower left, "poor trait of radon," reinforces the irony of drawing a portrait of something invisible. The commentary is not overtly political or concerned with social change, but instead expresses Wiley's concern for the environment through an irreverent sense of humor.

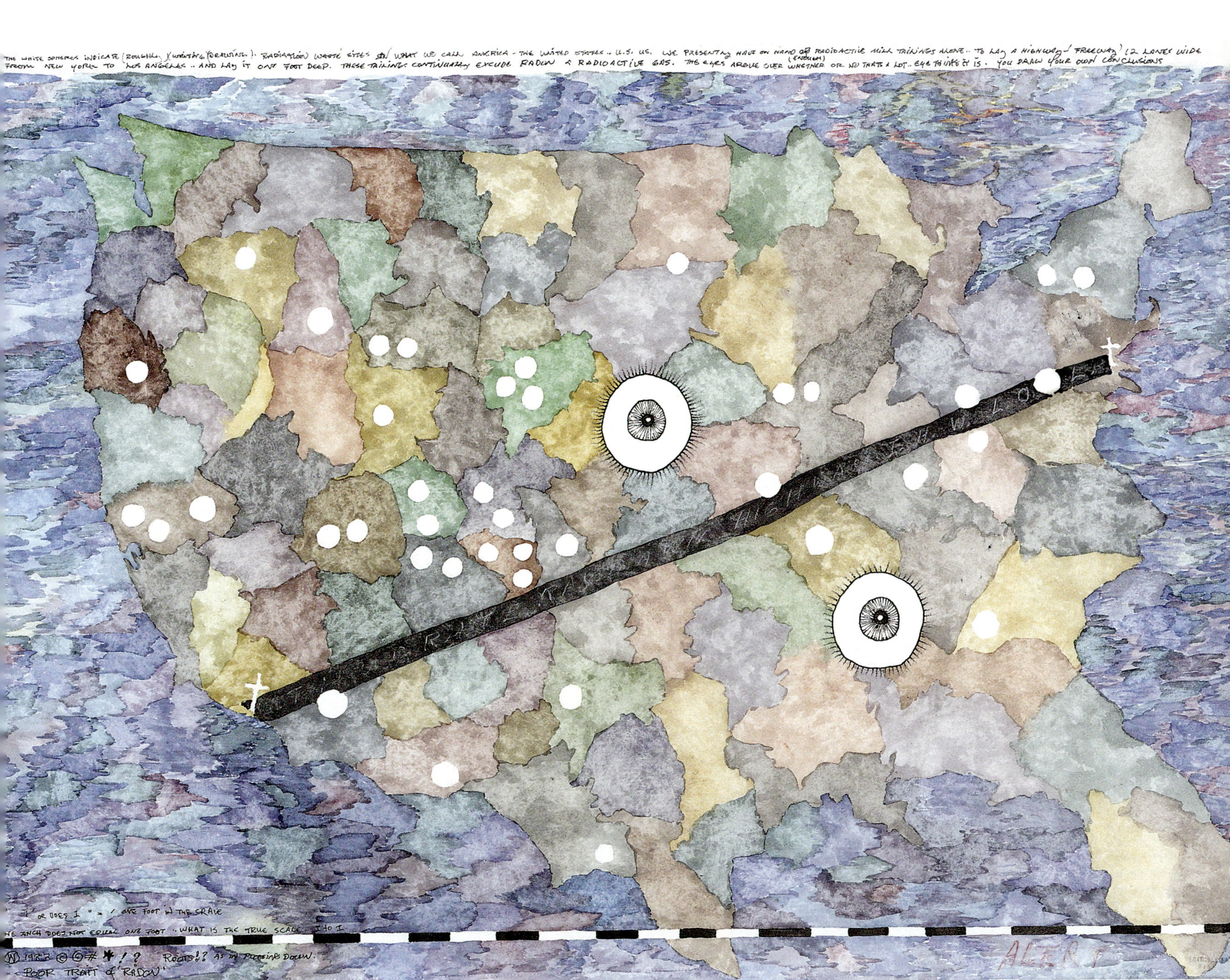
THE WHITE SPHERES INDICATE (ROUGHLY (WRITING) (DRAWING)). RADIATION WASTE SITES IN WHAT WE CALL AMERICA - THE UNITED STATES .. U.S. US. WE PRESENTLY HAVE ON HAND (ENOUGH) OF RADIOACTIVE MILL TAILINGS ALONE .. TO LAY A HIGHWAY (FREEWAY) 12 LANES WIDE
FROM NEW YORK TO LOS ANGELES .. AND LAY IT ONE FOOT DEEP. THESE TAILINGS CONTINUALLY EXCUDE RADON A RADIOACTIVE GAS. THE EYES ARGUE OVER WHETHER OR NO THATS A LOT .. EYE THINK IT IS. YOU DRAW YOUR OWN CONCLUSIONS
1' OR DOES 1" = 1 ONE FOOT IN THE GRAVE
ONE INCH DOES NOT EQUAL ONE FOOT .. WHAT IS THE TRUE SCALE 1 to 1
1983 ©#*!? ROOTS!? AS IN PUTTING DOWN.
POOR TRAIT OF "RADON"
ALERT

**ANDREW WYETH**

born 1917

# *November First*

1950
watercolor
21 ¾ x 29 ¾ in.
Smithsonian American Art Museum, Bequest of Winifred M. Jacobson

Andrew Wyeth has steadfastly maintained his dedication to painting the people and places that are familiar to him in Chadds Ford, Pennsylvania, and Cushing, Maine. The cornfield depicted in this watercolor is located near his studio in Chadds Ford, behind the house of Dr. Margaret Handy, the pediatrician who cared for Wyeth's two children.

Shocked by the sudden death of his father in a railroad crossing accident in 1945 and disturbed by his own serious illness in 1950, Wyeth turned away from what he has called the clever "swish and swash" of his early watercolors to solemn, spare meditations on the responsiveness of nature and the cycles of life. Depicting tattered cornstalks in a harvested field, *November First* not only captures the cold damp of late autumn, but elicits thoughts on the land's inevitable patterns of decay and renewal. The quick, sure brushstrokes reveal his noted facility with watercolor, a medium Wyeth appreciates for its spontaneity.

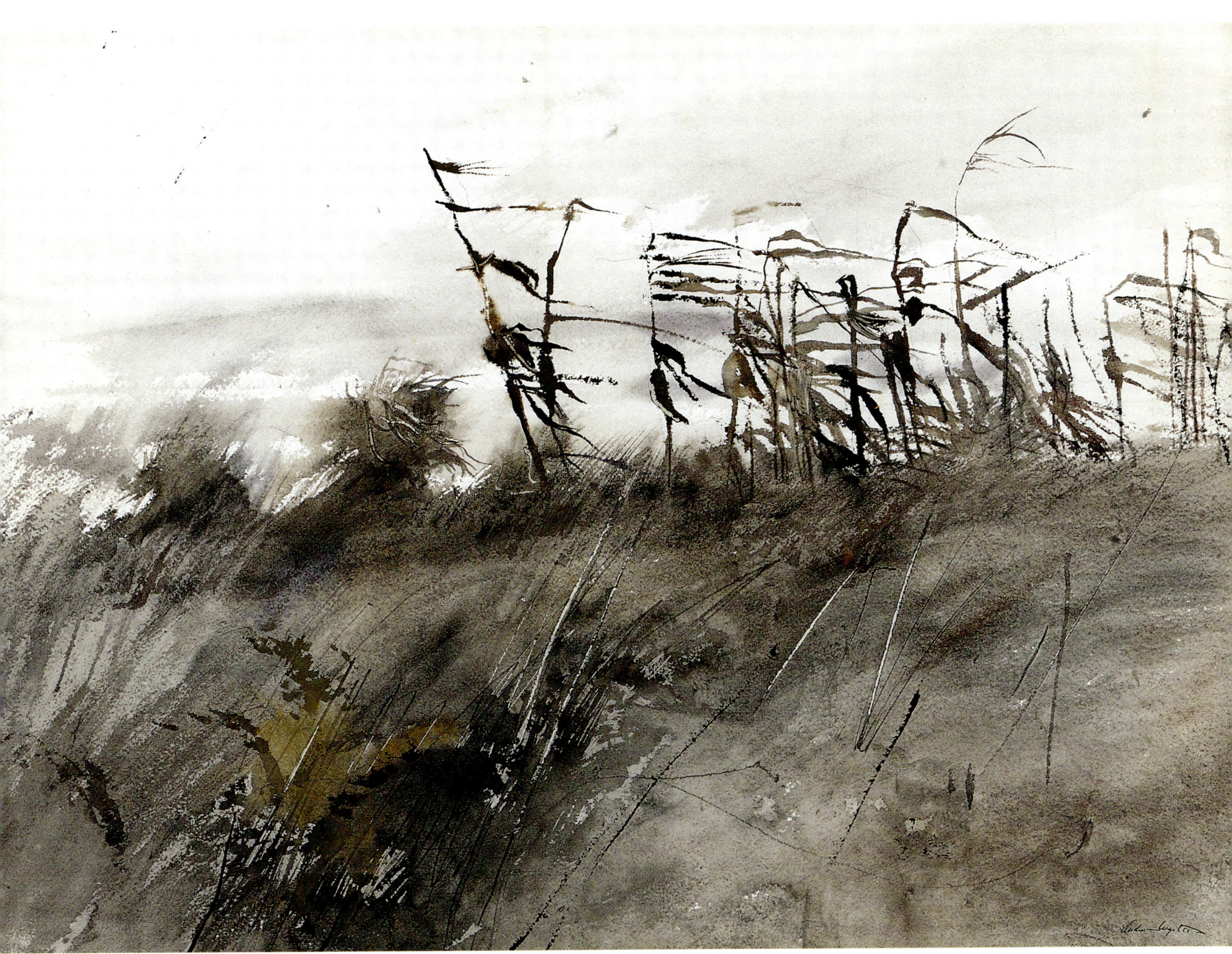

**MARGUERITE ZORACH**

1887–1968

## *Zoltan Hecht*

1913
watercolor and pencil
11 x 8 ½ in.
Smithsonian American Art Museum

Marguerite Zorach was more interested in the expressive qualities of colors than their accuracy. In her portrait of Zoltan Hecht, the red-orange eyebrows, bright green eyes, and yellowish outline of his face and hands were arbitrary and not descriptive of the actual person. Hecht was a fellow modernist artist who had helped her husband hang his first solo exhibition in Cleveland. She shows him as a relaxed, thoughtful, and dapper fellow, suggesting his affiliation with the modernist movement in her choice of bright, unconventional colors.

When Zorach returned to the United States in 1912 from several years of studying art in Europe, her friends and family ridiculed the modernist style she had adopted in Paris. They were especially appalled by the liberties she took with color, which art critics described with sarcastic glee. What her detractors failed to appreciate was her sensitive draftsmanship, economy of line, and eloquent compositions that captured the feeling of the subject.

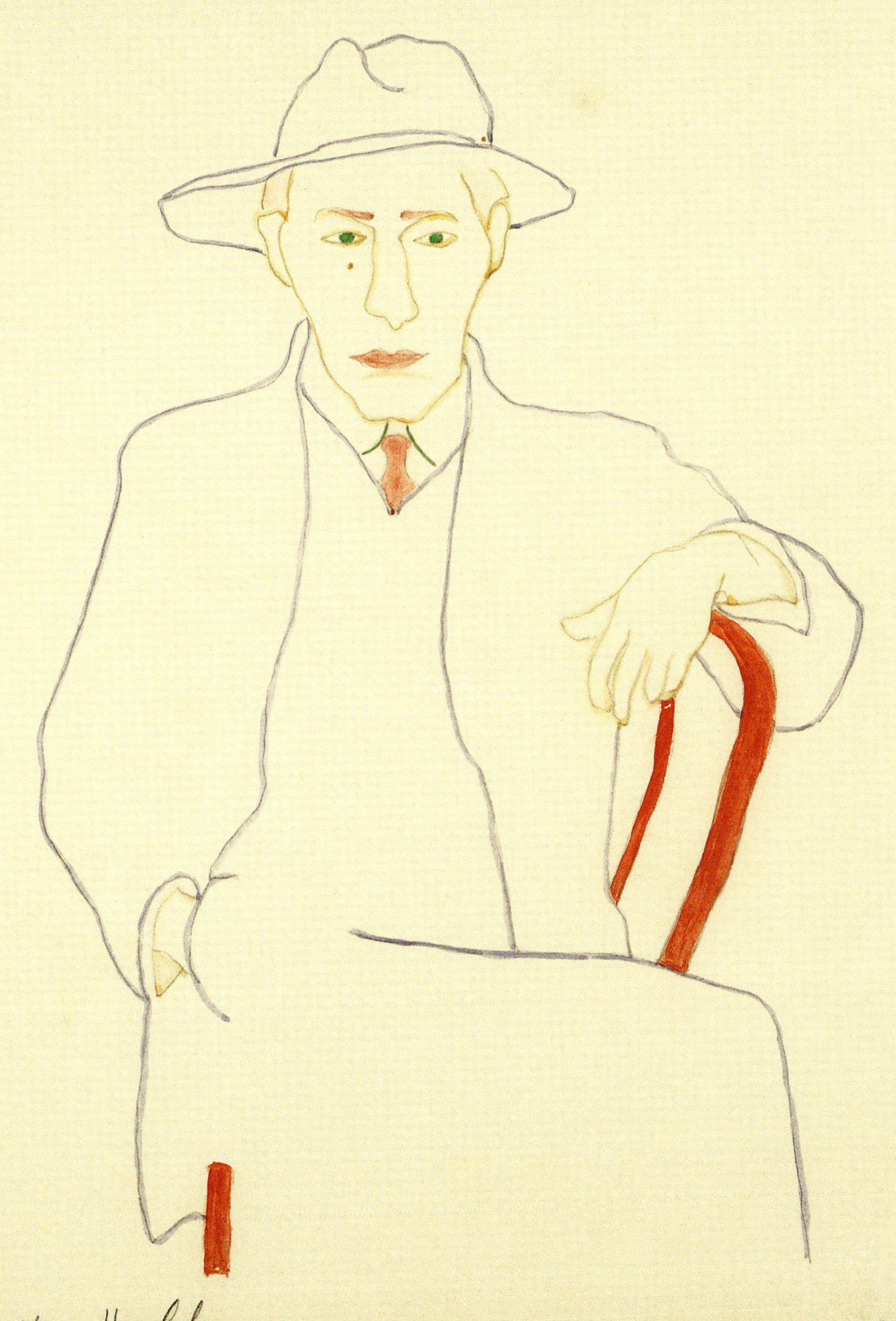
Zoltan Hecht
M. Zorach

# Index of Titles

# *Sources of Quotations*

p. 18: Irene McManus, *Carolyn Brady* (Rockland, Maine: The William A. Farnsworth Library and Art Museum, 1987), n.p.

p. 20: Adelyn D. Breeskin, *Romaine Brooks* (Washington: Smithsonian Institution Press, 1986), 38

p. 24: Paul Cadmus, *Quotes and Notes* for Subway Symphony, exhibition brochure (New York: Midtown Galleries, 1976), n.p.

P. 30: Diane Kelder, ed., *Stuart Davis* (New York: Praeger, 1971), 80

p. 32: Gary Gildner, "Where the Wild Beasts Come From," in *Wild Beasts: Roy De Forest and Gaylen Hansen* (Great Falls, Mont.: Paris Gibson Square Museum of Art, 1999), 5

p. 38: Susan A. Hobbs, *The Art of Thomas Wilmer Dewing* (Washington: Smithsonian Institution Press, 1996), 201

p. 40: Kristine McKenna, "April Gornik: The Allure of the Dark Side," *Los Angeles Times,* 20 May 1990

p. 46: SAAM curatorial files

p. 64: Robert Jarvis, "Pictures by La Farge," *Art Amateur* 2 (June 1884): 13

p. 66: Louis Lozowick, "*Gas.* A Theatrical Experiment," *Little Review* 11, no. 2 (winter 1926): 59

p. 80: Gail Levin, "The Natural Magic of Charles Seliger," in *Charles Seliger: Nature's Journal* (New York: Michael Rosenfeld Gallery, 1994)

p. 84: AAA, The David Smith Papers—Speeches. Newcomb College, Tulane University, March 21, 1955

p. 86: Selden Rodman, *Conversations with Artists* (New York: The Devin-Adair Co., 1957), 182

p. 88: Joseph Stella, "Discovery of America: Autobiographical Notes," *Art News* (November 1960): 66

p. 90: Dewey F. Mosby, *Henry Ossawa Tanner* (Philadelphia: Philadelphia Museum of Art, 1991), 176

p. 92: Henry T. Hopkins, *California Painters: New Work* (San Francisco: Chronicle Books, 1989), 125; letter from Nick Ward to Merry Foresta, 8 December 1989, SAAM curatorial files

p. 96: Selden Rodman, *Conversations with Artists* (New York: The Devin-Adair Co., 1957), 18

p. 102: "Maker of Curious Pictures in Town; Weber Modestly Unburdens His Soul and Discusses His Rivals," *Baltimore Evening News,* March 1915; cited in Phylis Burkley North, "Max Weber: The Early Paintings (1905–1920)" (Ph.D. diss., U. of Delaware, 1975), 172n.8

p. 106: Richard Meryman, "Andrew Wyeth," *Life* 58 (May 14, 1965): 108